C000131592

ALL ABOUT CRYSTALS
Connie Islin
ISBN 965-494-111-2

ALL ABOUT TAROT
Hali Morag
ISBN 965-494-062-0

ALL ABOUT THE WICCA OF LOVE
Tabatha Jennings
ISBN 965-494-110-4

ALL ABOUT THE SIXTH SENSE
Tom Pearson
ISBN 965-494-138-4

ALL ABOUT NUMEROLOGY
Lia Robin
ISBN 965-494-109-0

ALL ABOUT PALMISTRY
Batia Shorek
ISBN 965-494-094-9

ALL ABOUT DREAMS
Eili Goldberg
ISBN 965-494-061-2

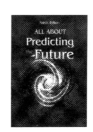

ALL ABOUT PREDICTING THE FUTURE
Sarah Zehavi
ISBN 965-494-093-0

ALL ABOUT SYMBOLS
Andrew T. Cummings
ISBN 965-494-139-2

ALL ABOUT CHAKRAS
Lily Rooman
ISBN 965-494-149-X

LIMIT OF LIABILITY

The accuracy and completeness of the information contained in this book and the opinions stated herein are not guaranteed or warranted to produce any particular results, and the advice and techniques contained herein may not be suitable for every individual. Neither the publisher nor the author shall be liable for any loss of profit or any other damages, commercial or other, including but not limited to special, incidental, consequential, or other damages.

The information in this book is not meant to serve as a substitute for expert medical advice or treatment. It is designed to help you make informed choices. Since every individual is unique, a professional health care provider must diagnose conditions and supervise treatment for each individual health problem. If an individual is under a physician's care and receives advice that is contrary to the information provided in this book, the physician's advice should be followed, because it is based on the unique characteristics of that individual.

ALL ABOUT

Chakras

Lily Rooman

Knowing and activating the
body's energy centers

Astrolog Publishing House Ltd.

Cover design: Na'ama Yaffe

© Astrolog Publishing House 2002

ISBN 965-494-149-X

All rights reserved to Astrolog Publishing House Ltd.

P. O. Box 1123, Hod Hasharon 45111, Israel

Tel: 972-9-7412044

Fax: 972-9-7442714

E-Mail: info@astrolog.co.il

Astrolog Web Site: www.astrolog.co.il

All rights reserved. No part of this publication may be reproduced, stored in a retrieval system, or transmitted, in any form or by any means, electronic, mechanical, photocopying, recording or otherwise, without the prior permission of the publisher.

Published by Astrolog Publishing House 2002

10 9 8 7 6 5 4 3 2 1

❀ CHAKRAS ❀

contents

 CHAKRAS

The energetic system and the subtle bodies

Beyond what we can easily see and touch – material matter – is the electromagnetic field – the aura – and the subtle bodies, which are composed of thin, subtle, energetic matter. A well-known law of physics states that energy never disappears – it just changes form. As the physical body dies and continues the cycle of life through decomposition and composition, so our more subtle bodies do not disappear, but ostensibly change their form. This is the force that drives the person – body, mind, and spirit. When the spirit departs the body, the flesh, which was once active and creative, is left lifeless.

Our being is activated by a complex and complicated energetic system, without which the life and existence of the physical body would not be possible. This system includes the subtle energetic bodies, the chakras or the energy centers, and the meridians or the energy channels. In addition, a vast, indefinable universal force activates and directs our soul. The energetic bodies, chakras, and meridians function as valves which "reduce" the tremendous life force that we are incapable of receiving in all its power. We can only take it in small doses – each person according to his own capacity.

The aura

The aura is the electromagnetic field that surrounds the human body as well as every organism and object in the universe. When, for example, we see paintings of Christian saints with a circle of white or yellow light around their heads, or angels with their halos, we can see how people imagined the electromagnetic field looked. This is not just the imagination of the painters and artists, however, and these auras do not only surround saints or angels. The aura itself frequently resembles those in these paintings. It surrounds every creature, and every person, but the higher the person's energetic cleanliness and level of spiritual connection to the higher, divine energy levels, the higher the frequencies at which his electromagnetic field vibrates, creating the feeling of a "radiant" face, or "luminous" eyes. All of us, without exception, as well as the various animals, plants, and objects, are surrounded by electromagnetic fields of varying strength.

The electromagnetic field – the aura – has been known to people for many years. Through the ages, mystics, healers, shamans, clairvoyants, and people with supernatural powers have been able to feel and see the electromagnetic field around the human body. Many ancient sources, including the "Zohar" (the Book of Splendor) in the Jewish tradition and many ancient mystical works tell of the aura and relate to it in different ways. In general, however, there is an exceptional consensus among the ancient writers about the effect of external and internal influences on it, about what it symbolizes, and about its size and colors – even though the writers came from different places and encompassed most of the peoples of the world.

In the twentieth century, with the development of science, more and more scientists began to take an interest in the mysteries of the electromagnetic field. Michael Farraday, Nikola Tesla, and Thomas Edison were among the many scientists who encountered the electromagnetic field surrounding the human body during their experiments, and were astounded at their discoveries. But it was only in the fourth decade of the twentieth century, a time when many scientists started performing pre-planned experiments in order to comprehend and discover the nature of the electromagnetic field, that the entire subject was given a significant push forward. The best-known of these scientists is the Russian, S. D. Kirlian, who developed Kirlian photography, a technology which can record the electromagnetic field of living organisms. Today, this method of documentation is called "electro-photography." Electro-photography uses a phenomenon called "aura emission." The aura is the result of electron emission. In electro-photography, millions of electrons are emitted and move toward a special part of the camera, which absorbs them, creating magnificent and beautifully colored pictures of the patterns of energy emission.

In Kirlian photography, the feet and hands of the subject are usually photographed. The feet and hands are briefly exposed to high-frequency rays on the surface of the photographic plate, and the result is documented on the plate or photographic paper. When the plate or paper is developed, a magnificent picture of the electromagnetic field surrounding the hands or feet is revealed; astonishingly, the tip of each finger or toe has its own unique electromagnetic field. Surprisingly, Kirlian photography reinforced many theories concerning reflexology and acupuncture. When a certain area on the foot or hand, especially at the tips of the digits, had a weak, blocked, or punctured aura, it turned out that there were problems with the meridian that was linked to this point or reflex area (it could be any organ in the body). The development of the use of Kirlian photography solved many mysteries connected to our electromagnetic field, and gave a significant boost to complementary medicine. The photographic "proof" that every object in the universe is surrounded by an electromagnetic field stunned many people. Others saw in it concrete corroboration of what they believed or even felt and saw.

The publication of these works, findings, and research gave rise to an increase in interest and the desire to understand the electromagnetic field that surrounds the human being, and its effects on his sensations.

Concurrently, the ability to understand the action of the electromagnetic field increased, as did the ways to positively influence its condition.

The electromagnetic field that surrounds every object can be positive or negative, perfect or deficient. But it is not static and immutable, or unaffected by external and internal factors. It is extremely dynamic and operates interactively with various internal and external factors. The organisms in the universe live in a perpetual state of energetic "give and take" among the various energetic fields, and they have to safeguard their electromagnetic fields against harm by negative or "energy-draining" electromagnetic fields. A great deal of research has shown that plants, for instance, shrink when there is negative or hostile energy in the vicinity of their electromagnetic field. Human beings are liable to feel the same way when they are in the presence of non-positive energy that emanates from various places, people, or objects. Occasionally, this sensitivity is translated into a "gut feeling" that causes us to move away from a certain place or person, or, conversely, to be attracted toward certain places, situations, or people. Incompatibility between the electromagnetic fields of various people, or between a person and surroundings of some kind sometimes causes a feeling of inexplicable discomfort.

Sometimes, we find ourselves desperate to get away from certain people or places because of the lack of equilibrium that appears in their electromagnetic fields, because of an energetic incompatibility, or because one of the auras is too strong and dominant, emits non-positive frequencies, and so on. Although this feeling often does not have a conscious explanation, the information about the electromagnetic field of a certain person, environment, or object is picked up by our electromagnetic field. These messages pass through the electromagnetic field to the nervous system and affect the person's general feeling. Sometimes, they appear as signs that warn us to get away from the particular environment or person whose energy is not in harmony with ours, or is liable to harm our energetic equilibrium in some way. These signs will probably be expressed as a feeling of discomfort, agitation, rejection, anxiety, and so on.

Animals are extremely sensitive to electromagnetic fields. While their natural sensitivity does not exceed ours (although it does not always operate according to the same mechanisms), they react directly to the feeling of energy and to the messages they pick up. It is absolutely true that dogs and cats can sense energy that is non-positive or unsuitable for them in their surroundings, or sense the energetic type of person near them. The biochemical explanations for these feelings in animals are correct. However, they constitute merely a part of the feelings to which animals react (that is, they explain the phenomenon on the biochemical level, which is an addition to the energetic layer, and not a substitute for it), and only explain the phenomenon partially.

Every person, without exception, has the ability to sense electromagnetic fields, as well as see different levels of these fields, if he is conscious of this possibility and perseveres in developing it. The reason why most people do not see or feel them is that these senses, similar to the more physical senses (smell, hearing, etc.), are not sufficiently developed, and are even perhaps atrophied. The inability of many people to conceive of seeing something that they have never seen in a physical manner also has an inhibiting effect – to the point that the disbelief in the existence of the electromagnetic field is liable to affect their ability to see it.

Clairvoyants are able to discern the aura, and so are people who have honed their extrasensory visual powers. By observing the aura, it is possible to see that it contains different colors. Some of the colors are relatively "fixed." Others are changeable. The sum total of the colors may fade or intensify according to the person's mood and emotional, mental, and physical states. Of course, the person's spiritual state also has an enormous effect on the colors and size of the aura.

The main part of the color and energy in the aura is provided and activated by the action of the chakras.

In general, the aura spreads over a distance of 10-15cm from the physical body, and includes a number of energetic layers that are called the energetic bodies ("the subtle bodies").

The layers of the body – the energetic bodies

The layers of the body are other subtle bodies that exist around the physical body. Each one of these bodies, of which there are claimed to be four, five, six or even seven, has its own unique frequency. The ethereal body – the one that is closest to the physical body – has the lowest frequency. The astral and mental bodies have higher frequencies, while the spiritual body, and the bodies that are even higher than that have the highest frequencies.

It is very common for a person to sense somebody standing behind him, or beside him, without touching him – he feels a kind of touch, despite the physical distance. This is because the energetic bodies, all of which have their own "auras," are situated at different distances from the body, and are spread over broader areas than the physical body. Consequently, they may come into contact with the electromagnetic field of another person. The frequencies of the energetic bodies, their magnetic and electric current, dictate the person's electromagnetic field (aura) at different levels. Each one of the bodies has its own auric layer, and altogether, they constitute the electromagnetic field that contains all the information about us – our past, present, and future.

The bodies of the aura are in a perpetually interrelated system, and affect one another as well as the person's feelings, emotions, thinking, behavior, and health. As a result, a state of imbalance in one of the bodies leads to a state of imbalance in the others. Similarly, the development of the person's spirit and awareness affects the frequencies of each of the energetic bodies. When the frequencies of the bodies rise, this has an effect on the person's entire being – he becomes more energetic and vital, and is able to pick up and absorb higher energy frequencies, which affect the development of his spirit and awareness. This is how the perpetual interaction between the person's awareness and the state of his energetic bodies operates.

The physical body

The physical body is the first body. It is the "thickest" of all the bodies, tangible and material, visible and palpable. Our physical body works on the given physical levels, and is largely subject to the known physical laws. It comprises matter – atoms, cells, tissues, and organs. It is activated and controlled by various biochemical processes, and requires physical nourishment, motion, and evacuation. Perpetual destructive and regenerative processes occur simultaneously in it. When the person is young and his body is growing, the anabolic (building) forces operate more strongly than the catabolic (destructive) forces. This gradually changes as the body ages.

However, in spite of all this, if we look at things in depth, the physical body is far from being "physical," material, and absolutely stable. Our bodies, like the other objects in existence, are made up of atoms. Atoms are not stable and motionless – on the contrary. Atoms are in a state of perpetual motion, it is their density that creates the state of matter: solid, liquid, or gas. An astounding finding of quantum physics research revealed that the atom itself is changeable! Sometimes it behaves as a particle, and sometimes as a wave. The meaning of this incredible finding is that atoms are not just physical and stable, but also energetic. This means that we live in two worlds simultaneously.

The ethereal body

The ethereal body is the second body, and the first conscious body. It is also called the aura of the body. It is reminiscent of the physical body in shape, which is why it is sometimes called "the ethereal twin" or "the inner physical body."

The ethereal body carries inside it the forces that shape the physical body, the life energy that creates motion, and all the physical senses. The physical human body is nourished, develops, and exists through this more subtle energy field, and diseases begin their path to physical manifestation in it. For this reason, by treating the ethereal body, it is possible to treat physical conditions, since the ethereal body is a subtle bio-field that penetrates all matter. This subtle body is responsible for the person's general health and diverse activities. It carries within it the meridians, and they convey life energies and charge the body with energy.

Although the ethereal body is indiscernible to normal observation (with a little effort, however, it is possible to develop the ability to see it), it is composed of a material that belongs to the physical world, but it is invisible because it vibrates at a higher level than matter does. Frequently, we absorb and grasp it unconsciously. It is described as a misty material that surrounds the body at a distance of 2.5-10cm.

The ethereal body channels emotions (that affect and are affected by the emotional body), thoughts and intuitions (that are linked to the mental body) and spiritual information. Ultimately, the sum total is expressed in the material world.

The ethereal body is recreated in every incarnation, and dissipates a few days after the death of the physical body. It draws its energy from the sun via the solar plexus chakra and from the earth via the base chakra. It stores these energies and nourishes the physical body with them through the chakras and the meridians. These two forms of energy – sun energy and earth energy – ensure a living and breathing balance in the body's cells. When the body's need for energy is satisfied, the ethereal body liberates excess energy via the chakras and the pores in the skin, and it moves to a distance of 2.5-10cm from the physical body. In this way, an ethereal aura is created around the body. As we said before, this aura is the easiest one to see when we practice seeing the aura, and it is generally the first one we succeed in seeing. The rays of energy that leave the body envelop it in a protective layer. This layer protects the body against bacteria and viruses that are disease carriers, as well as against harmful substances, and safeguards its health. At the same time, it radiates life energy to the environment.

When we examine the protective quality that the ethereal layer creates, it is easy to understand that when the ethereal body is in optimal condition – or even slightly less – there is little chance that the person will succumb to a disease from the outside. In a case like this, the reason for the disease, if there is one, will stem from inside. These reasons can include negative thoughts, non-positive emotions, an unharmonious and stressful lifestyle, an unhealthy way of life, not paying heed to and not fulfilling the body's needs properly, and, of course, ingesting harmful substances such as nicotine, alcohol, and so on. All of the above use the strength of the ethereal body and exploit its energy stores, so that the body's protective sheath weakens, and gradually the window to "catching" external diseases opens. This is how "weak" areas and "holes" are formed in the aura. The flow of energy leaving the body so as to create an energetic sheath around it looks "distorted" instead of straight, or "confused" and unharmonious. This is how hollows, holes, or – in contrast – centers in which a great deal of energy accumulates and gets stuck are created in the human aura. This state enables negative energy and various external diseases, viruses, and bacteria to penetrate the person's physical body.

The problem does not end there, however. In addition, essential energy is liable to "leak" through the holes or gaps in the energetic sheath. This is how it is possible to identify states of disease by observing or feeling the ethereal body even before they manifest themselves in the physical body itself. Moreover, it is possible to treat them while they still exist only in the ethereal body by administering treatment to this body.

The ethereal body constitutes a body that connects the high energetic bodies to the physical body. It transmits information that is obtained through our physical senses to the mental and astral bodies, and simultaneously transmits energy and information from the superior bodies to the physical body. When the energy of the ethereal body is weakened, this communication may be harmed, and the person may feel indifferent and unconcerned mentally and emotionally.

The ethereal body, and similarly the physical body, reacts well to thoughts that are transmitted via the mental (conceptual) body. For this reason, work with mantras or positive affirmations has such a powerful effect on the health of the body.

Kirlian photography revealed that plants, especially trees and flowers, radiate a very similar energy to that radiated by the ethereal body. This is apparently one of the reasons that plants help us replenish our energy supply so powerfully, in different ways and forms. This energy can be found in aromatic oils, Bach flowers, and various medicinal herbs. When the person is outdoors, the plant kingdom pours this beneficial energy onto him, and it strengthens and renews his powers.

The astral (emotional) body

The astral body is the second energetic body, and it is also called the emotional body. This body carries within it all of our emotions, as well as the characteristics of our nature. It is directly affected by emotions, and it affects them. When the person is not particularly mature emotionally and spiritually, it is possible to make this body out as a kind of untidy cloud that moves in different directions. The more mature the person is in his emotions, thoughts, and character traits, the clearer and more defined the shape of his astral body will appear.

The astral body's aura is oval, and surrounds the body at a distance of 30-40cm. Every emotional change, every state of emotional imbalance, is projected to the entire aura via the astral body. This process is performed mainly by the chakras, and to a small extent by the pores in the skin. Outwardly, the person's emotional state is projected to the environment, and it is easy to discern, using our senses, when the person is angry, depressed, agitated, or upset, even if he seems indifferent. Sensitive people have no difficulty feeling the environmental effect of emotional projection when it is not balanced, and some of them feel disturbed and uncomfortable when they are in the vicinity of a person projecting non-positive emotions. Extremely sensitive people are liable to feel like this when a person is calm and relaxed, but at the same time carries various residual non-positive emotions from different times and events.

The astral aura is in perpetual motion. Because a person's basic character traits are expressed in the aura via basic colors, the astral aura is likely to change according to the person's emotions and emotional state.

For this reason, the colors of the astral body are perpetually changing. Negative emotions such as anger, depression, fear, and worry are expressed in dark colors and patches on the surface of the aura. In contrast, when the person feels love, happiness, joy, confidence in the universe, and courage, bright, variegated, "clean," shining colors can be discerned on his aura.

Of all the auras, one can say that the astral aura is the one that most powerfully shapes the average person's world-view and the reality in which he lives. The astral body contains all the unresolved emotional conflicts, all the repressed emotions, the conscious and unconscious fears, the fears and emotions of rejection, the feelings of loneliness, aggressiveness, and lack of self-confidence. This emotional mass transmits its vibrations via the astral body to the world by sending unconscious messages to the universe.

This is extremely significant – these messages that we send to the world consciously or unconsciously via the astral body, are the ones that attract a certain reality to our lives. What we send is what we ultimately receive. Transmitting negative emotions brings negative events into our lives, thus fulfilling the (conscious or unconscious) pessimistic prophecies that invited these events in the first place. The energetic vibrations we transmit attract identical or similar energetic vibrations from the environment. Therefore, we repeatedly encounter situations, events, or people that constitute a mirror image of what we repress, fear, or want to get rid of.

However, this situation of a "mirror" meeting with people around us or with events that occur in our lives has a purpose. The unresolved emotions that are contained in our astral body are in a constant state of wanting to disappear. When we repeatedly encounter events or people who act as a mirror for us, it is another opportunity for us to resolve these emotions. When we consciously work on these emotions, we are once again placed in the situation that acts as a mirror for the unresolved conflicts within us – but now we confront the situation courageously and deal with it wisely, and those feelings may well disappear and leave our emotional body.

The mental body, and its conscious thoughts, has a certain influence on the astral body, but it is relatively minor. Just as the subconscious may create its system of laws and conventions, so the astral, emotional body works according to its laws. A very simple example may be seen in the person who repeatedly says that there is no reason to be afraid of the cockroach that is scuttling around on the floor. Only very rarely does this repetition have any practical effect on the person's fear. Intellectual thought has the ability to direct external behavior, but does not significantly affect the subconscious, except via various mantras of positive thinking that address the subconscious directly and change old patterns within it.

In the emotional body, we find all the old beliefs and emotional patterns that we have accumulated between childhood and maturity. Old wounds from our childhood reside there, as well as emotions of rejection, feelings of worthlessness, and various other non-positive patterns that we created about ourselves. These old patterns clash with our conscious world over and over again. A common conflict, for instance, is where a person yearns to love and be loved, but does not understand what is standing in his way. Why does love not burst into his life, or why does it repeatedly slip through his fingers? It is very likely that the unconscious belief that he is not worthy of love, or that he is incapable of love – a belief whose origin may date back to his early childhood, or even to his infancy – resides in his astral body.

However, this situation does not begin and end just in this life. Unresolved feelings, emotional conflicts, and their repercussions on our lives and on our surroundings (via our world-view and our conduct), continue with us into our subsequent incarnations, until they are resolved. This is because the emotional body does not disintegrate when the physical body dies, but continues into the next body, in the next incarnation. Moreover, a store of unresolved experiences is likely, to a great extent, to shape our next incarnation, and the conditions of our life in it.

When we assimilate these laws of the universe, we understand that in fact our fate is in our own hands. We cannot blame events, and certainly not other people, because we ourselves brought these events into our lives, be it via the emotional mass that is embodied in the emotional body during our present life, or be it in previous incarnations.

Most of the emotional complexes are located in the area of the solar plexus chakra. Via this chakra, we react emotionally to the experiences that occur in our lives. If we want to be conscious, in a rational way, of the emotions that are raging inside us, we have to stimulate the third eye chakra, which characterizes the highest form of expression of the astral body, so that we can penetrate the contents of the solar plexus chakra. However, even after the conscious understanding of the deep, and formerly unconscious, feelings that rage inside us, we have to open our hearts and change those patterns through conscious behavior. To this end, we need to stimulate and open the heart and crown chakras. When our heart is open, and universal wisdom directs and leads us, we can make the necessary repairs to this incarnation, and significantly influence the astral body. By directing the superego, we can begin to observe and understand the various experiences that we undergo, and what they are trying to teach us. Now we can learn life's lessons in a way that is not derisive, judgmental, or fearful, but rather understanding, learning, and repairing.

When the person's developed state of awareness and his connection to his superego for increasing periods of time cause the frequencies of his spiritual body to unite with his astral (emotional) body, the frequencies of his astral body become faster and faster. The faster they become, the more the astral body discards "bundles" of non-positive emotions, unresolved conflicts, and negative experiences. In this way, we slough off negative memories whose source is in negative experiences, and feel forgiveness and understanding toward ourselves and others. The more non-positive experiences are discarded, the more the frequencies of the astral body are fortified. It emits and radiates love, pity, compassion, joy, and gaiety to the environment, and attracts similar energetic vibrations to the person.

The mental (conceptual) body

The mental body is the third energetic body. All our ideas, rational thoughts, and even some of our intuitive perceptions are born in the mental body. It contains our thought patterns and mental beliefs, and is influenced by them. The vibrations of the mental body are higher than those of the ethereal and astral bodies, and its structure is less dense. It is also oval in shape, and it spreads over a distance of about 40-60cm from the body. The greater the person's awareness and conceptual and spiritual development are, the more space this body will occupy in the general electromagnetic field.

In cases where the person's conceptual development is relatively low, it is possible to discern the appearance of a kind of milky white substance in the person's mental body. In such cases, its colors will be relatively lacking in variety, faded, and dull. The more balanced, creative, original, and full of life and love the person's thoughts are, the more the colors of the aura of this body will be vivid, rich, and glowing.

The mental body has an upper layer and a lower layer. Its lower frequencies are expressed in linear thinking of the rational mind, which examines and checks what the eye can see using ostensibly logical equations. This layer is activated by thoughts concerning physical life, and by processing the information that is transmitted via the physical senses. The information is transmitted to the astral body via the ethereal body. The astral body translates the information into emotions, and transmits them in this form to the mental body. The mental body reacts to the information received through verbal thought, according to the patterns that are characteristic of the person.

The astral body and its emotions have a very strong influence on the apparently "rational" insight that is expressed in the conceptual body. Various emotional conflicts, unresolved emotional messes, affect the formation of thought, so that ultimately the majority of thought is neither objective nor "natural" – but rather the conceptual reaction to information expressed by the emotions according to understood thought patterns. The conceptual reaction is based on the way in which we react to the world, and can sometimes be different from the objective facts to which we relate. In addition, certain situations are liable to cause confusion in the astral body (which transmits the information to the mental body) so that the mental body cannot react properly. In such cases, the thought process becomes "confused" by the flood of various unconscious feelings. In these cases, we are likely to notice that when we are speaking to a person, he reacts to what we're saying in an emotional way that is not to the point.

Thoughts of this kind, which arise in the mental body, usually concern everyday matters and various material issues, and are linked to our general feeling and our more physical fields of interest. In this process, the main aim of the mental body is to supply rational answers and solutions to various opinions and information. However, this is only a minor use of the abilities of the mental body. The original use of this energetic body is to enable us to ask questions about universal truths, to assimilate them, and to "attract" information from the spiritual body – the mental body can absorb lofty insights and information. These insights, which come from the spiritual energetic body, are said to unite with rational thought in the mental layers by supplying the person with a more profound, objective, and conscious world-view. When this unity occurs, the person is able to react, both conceptually and practically, according to the laws of the universe.

However, as we said before, in order to do this, the mental body's way of reacting has to be elevated so that it is less influenced by the unresolved emotional conflicts that reach it from the emotional layer along with the sensory information from the ethereal layer.

The mental layer contains all of our thought patterns. Often, we react according to these patterns, which are liable to be erroneous and irrelevant, instead of reacting rationally and objectively (which still does not constitute the highest use of the abilities of the mental body!). We must pay heed to the thought patterns that are stored in the mental layer.

Located in this body are the beliefs, opinions, prejudices, and thought patterns (inhibiting ones, too) that we have accumulated during our lives. These thought patterns are projected outward, and, similar to what happens in the interaction between the universe and the astral layer, this situation also affects the reality in which we live. The beliefs to which we adhere in our thinking, attract situations and events that are compatible with this thought pattern. This is expressed in all areas of life.

Intensive work on recognizing thought patterns, creating awareness of the way of thinking, and altering inhibiting and useless thought patterns can be very helpful in many situations in the person's life. Working toward changing thought patterns that reside in the mental body is done by working on the subconscious: autosuggestion, hypnosis, and so on. Suggestions such as these work both on the mental body and on the astral body, which created them in the first place. This is not a trivial matter. As human beings, our path toward shaping our lives and our world begins and is rooted in thought. Physical embodiment in the material world and tangible reality begin in thought. Thought can stimulate speech, which is one of the main human ways of interacting, and after speech comes deed, which may make a karmic "repair" or, conversely, cause "damage." But everything begins in thought. Even things that are apparently done without thought ultimately derive from the astral (emotional) and the mental (conceptual) layers. This is because besides the conscious thoughts that go through our mind seemingly consciously and "voluntarily", there is an enormous mass of thoughts and emotional thoughts, inner beliefs, and conscious or unconscious thought patterns that actively direct our deeds.

When the person succeeds in discovering and identifying inhibiting thought patterns, and works on cleansing his astral body (which immediately affects his mental body), he may well begin to feel the full action of the mental body, which constitutes a link to the knowledge coming from the spiritual body.

The knowledge that comes to us from the spiritual body expresses itself as intuitive feelings, as inner enlightenment, as an insight, a sound or a vision. When the mental layer is healthy and balanced, it translates these intangible visions into conscious thought that can be expressed in speech. This brings the person to a deeper awareness and understanding of what is happening in his life. He sees a "passage" to simple linear thought, of cause and effect. His perception is broader and he can examine in depth the profound and fundamental factors that cause various events.

Reaching this layer – the higher layer of the mental body – necessitates the cleansing and understanding of the astral body with all the emotions contained in it, detaching oneself from old thought patterns and discarding them, and stimulating the third eye chakra by linking it to the crown chakra, which is open to receiving divine knowledge.

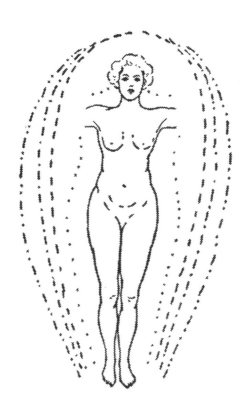

The spiritual (intuitive) body

The fourth conscious body is the spiritual body. It is also sometimes called the intuitive body, and some people call it or link it to the karmic body. The vibrations of this body are much higher than the vibrations of the other bodies, and it is the most subtle of all of them. In many people, this body is still undeveloped, or only partially developed. In people whose spiritual awareness is still undiscovered, the spiritual body does not extend a large distance from the physical body. In contrast, in a person who is spiritually developed and aware, the aura of the spiritual body may spread over a large distance, and its oval shape may turn into a perfect circle that encompasses the person with its light.

The spiritual body stores everything that is beyond what is defined as "rational", "logical", "cerebral." Through this body, the person receives intuitive messages, insights, and knowledge, and also experiences extrasensory perception and understanding, telepathic and prophetic dreams, "gut feelings," and prior knowledge.

The more balanced this body is, and the more aware and cognizant of it a person is, the easier it is to receive and decipher the intuitive messages that a person is receiving all the time, but is often unaware of. Alternatively, he may be aware of them, but he works against them.

It is possible to feel the spiritual body when we are in the presence of an enlightened, educated, just person, or true "maestro". When we are near him, we can feel a special feeling, which disappears when we move a certain distance away from him, leaving the area over which his aura extends. The feeling of these people's auras is a flow of love, peace, security, and tranquillity.

The aura of the spiritual body has a glowing and unique range of colors. This body frequently receives the highest energy, which, in order for it to be assimilated and understood, changes into lower frequencies that can be picked up by the mental, astral, and ethereal bodies. It makes itself compatible with the frequencies of these bodies, and helps them find the highest possible level of expression in their sphere. The way in which we receive, react, and store this energy depends on the state of our chakras.

Via the spiritual body, we experience a feeling of oneness with life, a feeling of connecting to God, to the universe, and to our fellow human beings, as well as to nature. When the person operates from his spiritual body, he acquires the ability to understand and access everything that exists in the universe.

This body is immortal. It is the divine part of us, while the other bodies are liable to change and even dissipate during our many incarnations.

Through the spiritual body, we can understand our objective in life, our vocation, and our existence in this world and in this incarnation. When connected to this conscious body, all of the person's actions stem from his higher self, and he operates perfectly according to the laws of the universe. Unconditional love flows in him, and affects his surroundings. Confidence, wisdom, power, and serenity accompany him constantly.

The spiritual body aspires, or is linked according to some people, to the additional body – the karmic body – about which very little is known. This body contains the knowledge concerning our vocation and the incarnations we have had, and our role as part of the universal whole.

The effects of the karmic body, or aura, are extremely important, but there aren't many people who know how to identify and understand them. They generally do so through channeling abilities, receiving superior messages, or the ability to discern the previous incarnations of the person, and the lesson he has to learn in this world and in this incarnation. Karmic effects are, for instance, handicaps, birth defects, serious deeds or crimes that are perpetrated against the person, severe mental illnesses, genetic diseases, perpetual poverty, and so on. Having said that, we have to remember the principle that everything is destined, but we do have freedom of choice. That means that despite the various karmic effects, the person can and must cope by balancing all his bodies; the aim of the karmic effects is to teach him how to cope with a certain situation in the most correct, connected, and pure way.

Because all the auras maintain a close interrelationship, a state of imbalance in one of the bodies has a direct effect on the other bodies. This point is very important when we set out to treat a particular disease or problem. Often, the physical problem can lead us to discover the basic imbalance that caused it, and is liable to continue creating situations of basic imbalance, until its root is treated. When we look at the problem holistically – that is, body, mind, and spirit together – we discover that in fact there is no "physical disease" or "mental disease" per se. Rather, every state of imbalance affects the various layers in one way or another, and is affected by them. When the person succumbs to a physical disease, or any other kind of disease, careful scrutiny reveals an imbalance in his other layers. In most cases, this imbalance is of the same type as the one that manifested itself physically. Often it is linked to the very chakra that affects both the particular mental state and the particular physical organs. In the same way, we can discover an imbalance in the various bodies, an imbalance that sometimes revolves around a certain point that will be manifested as some kind of physical disease in the physical body.

As an example, we will describe the possible source and development of a problem that is considered to be "easy" to describe from the point of view of its manifestation in the various layers. Constipation is a problem from which many people in the modern world suffer. It is clearly expressed in the physical body, and is liable to lead to many complications, such as excessive toxins in the digestive system, flatulence, chronically deficient digestion, and so on. When we examine the source of this disorder in the emotional-mental layer, we discover, theoretically, that constipation is an inability to let go. (This is in fact what happens in constipation!) It is possible that by looking at the person's characteristics, we will discover that he finds it difficult to let go of anything – money, possessions that he does not need, events from his past, and so on. When we observe his emotional behavior, we may see that he has difficulty letting go of emotions as well – he stops himself from expressing love, anger, or any other emotion, or finds it difficult to "let go" of various people in his life, and so on. If we observe his mental, conceptual behavior, we may see that he clings to old thought patterns that he "inherited" from his parents or from other people, and refuses to let go of them, although logically there is no point in clinging to them. This clinging to old, superfluous thought patterns is likely to be expressed in the intuitive layer as an inability to receive new knowledge and insights, to be open to various messages, or to heed his gut feeling, and in this way his intuitive abilities may be undermined. Of course, this is only an example (and each person must be related to individually by examining all of his problems and the properties of his personality and body), but it graphically demonstrates the interrelationship between our various bodies.

The problems, or imbalance, can start in any one of the bodies, but it is not easy to determine which preceded which – the chicken or the egg dilemma – if such "precedence" exists in the first place, since, as we said previously, the interrelationship is extremely close.

All of these problems, or states of imbalance or disharmony, constitute expressions of blockages in the person's bodies. In the same way as the blood, for instance, requires healthy, flexible arteries and veins in order for it to flow smoothly, so the flow of energy needs free and healthy "channels" without blockages. The correct flow of energy – a natural and smooth flow – will bring about balance on every level, and, of course, brings the person physical, mental, and spiritual health.

Free channels of energy are important and significant. When these channels are balanced, the person's ability to absorb and receive energy also depends on the balance and harmony between the bodies. When we observe the clever way in which we have been built, physically and energetically, in order to be a "vessel" or a "transmitter" of life energy (which is also called "chi") the question arises: What is the source of this energy that activates, affects, and realizes our being?

In the past, various philosophers tended to think, on the basis of mainly theoretical premises, that energy is located inside the person, and the person in fact constitutes a "closed circuit" from the energetic point of view, and nourishes and balances himself through his own self-energy. In contrast, many cultures, religions, and thinkers believe that the source of energy is in a tremendous energetic force that exists everywhere, all the time, and in everything. Some people called this force "God", "The Great Spirit", "The Universal Force" and various other names, including attributing the source of energy to nature (which is also, of course, an embodiment of the universal force, or God). This force gives the person life, and affects his movement, exactly like it affects the movement of the stars and the spinning of the earth on its own axis, or the movement of atomic particles. This tremendous energy is what "seeps" into the inner being of the person, and the very fact of its being inside him makes him "divine" in a certain sense. This view, which is mainly based on spiritual experiments, as well as on scientific discoveries that describe it (albeit via different definitions), is the most accepted view among people who are involved with, see, or feel energies. The reason for this is simple: When the person develops the ability to observe the aura, he can often see how, in various situations, the person whose aura he is observing receives a "current" of energy of a certain shape from an external source. For instance, it is sometimes possible to see a line, sphere/s, or cone of light above the head of a person who is meditating, linked up, or praying.

In order to receive this energy, the person must be spiritually clean and pure, and feel a desire and deservedness to receive. He is supposed to (and deserves to) receive the exact "helping" of the energy that suits him at the given moment of his physical, mental, and spiritual development. Sometimes, people attempt to obtain more of this energy either by apparently materialistic expressions of "accumulating" or "hoarding" energy, or by attempts to draw more of the energy in its pure or more spiritual form. Drawing excessive amounts of energy by artificial means (such as drugs, for instance), is liable to cause a situation in which the person is unable to contain the amount of energy. The consequences can be negative or dangerous, exactly like getting an insufficient amount of energy is likely to manifest itself in various states of imbalance, such as fatigue, weakness, lack of vitality, and so on.

How is this energy channeled in a correct and harmonious way into our body, and how does the passage of energy and the connection between the various bodies work? We will find the answers further on in this book by understanding how the chakras operate.

Feeling the bodies

The various conscious bodies can be felt. Sometimes, feeling the bodies is done intuitively, through the development of spiritual awareness. It is also possible to do a few exercises to develop our ability to feel our energetic bodies – exercises that simultaneously strengthen the intuition and increase spiritual awareness.

Exercise 1: Sit or lie down comfortably. Ensure that your spine is straight. Relax all your muscles until you feel that your body is relaxed and calm. Start taking slow, comfortable, deep, abdominal breaths, while concentrating on releasing your body during exhalation. Begin to touch and feel your physical body. Feel your feet, your abdomen, pass your hands over your face, your chest, your knees. Feel your bones, the contact with your skin, your muscles. Go in deeper, in your mind's eye, and see yourself feeling your inner organs, which operate so harmoniously inside you. Using the power of your imagination, try to go in even deeper, and see in your mind's eye the cells and atoms that comprise you. Allow yourself some time to feel and see your physical body.

After a few minutes, begin to consciously connect to another part of you – your emotions. The emotions are not visible to the eye like the physical body and the external organs are, but can be felt in exactly the same way. Feel your emotions, the emotional energy that is in you now. What is the emotion that you are feeling? What is the feeling? In your imagination, bring up an irritating incident that happened recently. Imagine it in detail in front of your eyes. How do you feel? What feelings are you experiencing? How powerful are they? Ask yourself: How strong are the emotions at present (when you recall them) as opposed to their strength during the actual incident? Do you feel a difference? Connect to your physical body for a moment. How does your physical body feel when you imagine the irritating incident? Do you feel changes in your blood flow or in your muscle tension? Let the incident go; imagine it being cast into a distant sea, or any other place away from you. Calm down and relax your body.

Now see in your mind's eye a happy, moving, or exciting event that happened some time ago. Imagine all the details: the people, the smells, the sounds, the feeling that you experienced during those happy moments. Look inside yourself; how do you feel? What feelings and emotional energy are going through you? Connect to your physical body and feel how it reacts to the event. Do you feel an expansion in the heart or abdominal region? Are your mouth muscles being pulled upward? Breathe deeply and relax your body. You may feel a feeling of strength in your abdomen – power and action. Take a deep breath into your heart, feel how it opens, feel the tremendous love that is inside you, and let it flow and fill your entire being. These emotions exist inside you and around you all the time, even though you can't touch them physically.

After feeling the emotional body, close your eyes and begin to focus your attention on what's going on inside your head. Thoughts pass through; listen to them. Which thoughts are passing through your head? Listen to them attentively while they go through your head. Pay attention to how they pass, what their rate is. Are they "slippery," or are they "stable"? Do they come in a flood or in a trickle? What topics do they center on? You are capable of listening to your thoughts. Now, conduct an interesting experiment. Grab one of the thoughts and change it however you like. This is an amazingly simply process – but extremely powerful. You can observe your thoughts – therefore you are not your thoughts. You are a witness to them. You activate them and you can direct them. They do not control you; you can control them and direct them as you like.

Try and stay in this state of awareness for a few minutes. In this state, you are aware of your various bodies, you feel them, and you are a witness to them; notice that they are a part of you, and that you have the ability to intervene, control, and watch their actions.

Try to let the thoughts pass without relating to them or paying special attention to them. Try to remain relaxed, calm, and without thoughts for several minutes. Be aware of and attentive to the feelings that arise in you.

Practicing this exercise every now and then will help you reach a higher state of awareness of your conscious bodies, understand their action and the interrelationship between them, internalize your ability to control them, and take full responsibility for them.

Exercise 2: This is a very simple exercise for feeling the energy field, and develops the ability to feel the auric field and the energetic bodies. Despite its simplicity, it is very effective for strengthening the ability to feel energetically, and it is worthwhile practicing it until the natural sensation of feeling the aura becomes very easy. Sit comfortably. Take deep, slow breaths, and relax your body. Spread your arms out at your sides, and with a slow, circular movement, bring your arms toward each other, until they are 10-15cm apart. Begin to slowly move your palms near to each other and further apart, focusing on the sensation in them, without letting them touch, maintaining a distance of at least 7cm between them. When the energy field that surrounds each hand comes into contact with the energy field of the other hand, you will feel resistance, a magnetic feeling, or a slight prickling. These sensations are the "echoes" of the energetic action of the chakras in the hands.

Another way of doing the exercise is with a partner, when both of you move your palms toward one another and further apart in order to feel the energy field that surrounds each one of them.

The chakras

The meaning of the Sanskrit word "chakra" is "wheel." Traditional writings relate that there are 88,000 chakras in the human being, which means that there is almost no area in the human body that is not energetically sensitive on a regular basis! By virtue of his very being, man is a creature that is tuned for frequent reception and conversion of energy. Most of the chakras are extremely small, with minor functions in the energy system. About 40 secondary chakras out of all the abovementioned ones have a significant function. The important ones among them are situated in the region of the spleen, the nape of the neck, the palms, and the soles of the feet.

The best-known and most significant chakras are the seven main chakras that are located along the central line of the body, parallel to the spine. These chakras play an extremely important role in human functions, in all layers of existence. They are responsible for the person's physical, mental, and spiritual functions.

These seven chakras are located in the ethereal body. Their shape is slightly reminiscent of that of a flower with petals and a stem, and in the ancient Hindu writings, they were described as similar to the lotus flower. The petals on the chakras represent energetic paths and channels through which the energy reaches the chakras, from where it goes to the subtle bodies. The number of petals changes from four on the base chakra to close to a thousand on the crown chakra.

From the center of each chakra, a leaf-like stem goes into the spine and joins with it. In this way, it connects the chakra with the most important energy channel, the Sushumana, which rises up along the spine to the head.

The chakras are in a state of perpetual rotation and vibration. Their rotation is what attracts and repels energy, according to the direction of the turn.

The chakras revolve in a clockwise direction, to the right, or in a counter-clockwise direction, to the left. A turn to the right has a yang, male meaning. It represents willpower and activity, and in its less positive meaning, aggressiveness and hunger for power. A turn to the left has a yin, female meaning, and symbolizes acceptance and acquiescence, as well as the less positive meaning, weakness.

It is important to recognize the direction in which the chakra turns in various types of treatment.

Every one of the chakras contains all the color frequencies, but there is one dominant color frequency that affects it, in accordance with the main action and function of the chakra. The more balanced the person's condition, and the higher his level of development and awareness, the stronger and brighter the color frequencies of the chakra. The size and vibrations of the chakras determine the amount of energy that they can absorb from various sources.

The chakras absorb energies that reach them from the universe, from nature, from celestial entities, from people, and even from things. They absorb and transmit energy to and from the various energetic bodies, and from the life-giving universal force.

The two most basic forms of energy reach the human system from the base chakra and the crown chakra. These two chakras are linked by the Sushumana, which is connected to the rest of the chakras by their "stems." Through the stems, it provides the chakras with essential energy. At the same time, the Sushumana is also the channel through which the Kundalini energy is stimulated.

When the Kundalini is stimulated, its energy is converted into various frequencies for each of the chakras, according to their frequencies, roles, and functions. The energy is manifested via the lowest frequencies of the base chakra, and the highest frequencies of the seventh chakra, the crown chakra. The converted frequencies are conveyed to the subtle bodies and to the physical body, and are perceived by us as sensations, emotions, and thoughts.

Each of the chakras is expressed on the physical body in one of the endocrine glands that regulate physical and emotional processes in the body. The higher energies, cosmic energies, are channeled through the chakras to the person's physical body. This energy, which is also called life energy, and flows through the chakras, is of cardinal importance to our lives and physical, mental and spiritual health.

When a situation arises in which the energy does not flow harmoniously through the chakras, or when one of the chakras is blocked or open too wide, it results in an imbalance that is manifested in all areas of life. The imbalance in the chakra will also be expressed in the endocrine gland that is linked to it, and the delicate metabolic balance of the body will be upset.

All the conscious bodies (that we mentioned previously), as well as the material body and everything else that exists in the universe, have their own unique vibrational frequency. Ideally, all of the person's conscious bodies are supposed to be linked and connected harmoniously. If one of the conscious bodies is not linked to one of the other bodies, it will prevent the passage of information and energy between those bodies. For instance, when the mental (conceptual) body and the emotional body are disconnected, the person may be unable to express his thoughts, or his emotions. Like any other sophisticated "instrument," which works on the principle of receiving and giving (absorption and transmission), the person also needs centers for absorption, transmission, and conversion of energy. These centers are the chakras.

In the physical body, the chakras function as "transmitters." They transmit the currents that arrive from the higher, purer energy, which operates at higher frequencies of the energetic bodies, to the physical body, by "converting" the high frequency to a frequency that our physical body can utilize. In the same way that domestic use of electrical energy that is too high (that is, at a different voltage) is liable to cause a short circuit, so the non-conversion of the energy that operates at higher frequencies in people can cause a blockage.

The conscious body that absorbs and contains the person's soul is the spiritual conscious body, which is our divine side, and it links us to creation. From this body, the energy passes to the other conscious bodies, each of which has a different objective and vocation. For this reason, each conscious body requires energy of a different quality and frequency. On each "surface" there are stations that convert the energy for the next surface.

The entire universe is connected by a tremendous primeval force. This force is transmitted to every thing and creature according to its capacity, and in accordance with the frequencies that suit it from the physiological, emotional, intellectual, and spiritual points of view. When the energy makes its way from this vast, primeval force to the bodies that are located in the universe, its strength and power apparently decrease more and more, so that these bodies can absorb it (since they cannot tolerate even an iota of its full original strength).

The human body, and the universe as well, is built of different layers – a spiritual layer, an emotional layer, an intellectual layer, and of course a material layer. The difference between the human body and the "body" of the cosmos lies only in the length of their waves and frequencies. As a result, the divine force is found not only outside us, but also inside us. Since human beings are able to use the gift of the imagination, they can attune themselves intellectually, intuitively, or emotionally, to the various energetic bodies and the various layers of awareness, and change them. All the methods of expanding consciousness, such as positive thinking, guided imagery, meditation, and many others, do this.

Consciousness is a very powerful tool. It is not limited by matter, distance, or time, and can move within our multidimensional being via the different layers of awareness. These changes can occur frequently and quickly. For this reason, the body's energy centers are very important. Every chakra serves as a relay and transmitting station to a particular area of frequency or awareness. When attention is focused on one of the chakras, the person is mainly involved in fields for which the particular chakra is "responsible," consciously or unconsciously. Often, this can help us diagnose a problem or an imbalance in one of the chakras. The person is liable to manifest deficient functioning in a field that is clearly connected to the action of one or more of the chakras. He is likely to talk about this at length, focus on it, and even display emotional and physical signs that lead us to identify the deficient functioning of one of the chakras.

Concentrating on the problem does not help solve it – on the contrary. The greater the amount of energy invested in thought and emotion concerning the problem itself, the more the problem will grow, or stagnate. In contrast, concentrating on balancing the chakra itself will lead to the opposite – positive – results: balancing the chakra and correcting the general imbalance (physical, emotional, and spiritual) that stemmed from the chakra's deficient functioning.

Through their spiritual abilities, the rishis (sages) of ancient India received information about the human energy system. They wrote this information in vedas that contain ancient knowledge. In India, as in other ancient, enlightened cultures, the chakras are aligned to certain colors, elements, signs, and properties. The combination of these elements – for instance, looking at a particular shape in a particular color while saying a mantra that is attributed to a particular chakra – that are linked to the chakra creates a certain frequency that can link up to a certain element in the human body via a certain resonance. For example, the element of earth is linked to the sex glands, to the first chakra, to the planet Mars, to the color red, and to the ruby. This technique of combining the elements leads to general balance that positively affects the person.

This activity also works in the opposite direction. When a person focuses on a certain property, desire, or aspiration, allows it to control his life, and lives by it, a situation arises wherein he works, lives, and communicates more from within the chakra that is linked to the subject to which he attributes so much importance. This is a "chicken or egg" situation in which a certain perception, way of thinking, and way of behaving causes an imbalance in the chakras. This imbalance, in turn, is liable to cause the situation to become extreme. It is difficult to say whether the imbalance in the chakra is what caused the imbalance in behavior, thought, and emotion, or vice versa.

We can look at a common example of this imbalance. A person whose entire focus of interest is increasing his income and accumulating more and more money, property, and assets, spends the greater part of his days concentrating on everyday problems, material issues, and physical matters without paying any attention to his intellectual, mental, or spiritual development. This person's awareness is significantly concentrated on his first chakra, and most of his thoughts are focused on survival, safeguarding his income, and materialistic issues. When most of the person's thoughts focus on a particular chakra in an unbalanced way, this can be expressed in several ways. For instance, excessive concentration on the first chakra is liable to characterize a person with violent impulses and a lust for wealth or sex – and conversely, this powerful energy is likely to express itself in strong energies, in a powerful life force, in a celebration of life, and great vitality. Thus, concentration on a particular chakra, which ultimately creates a certain imbalance, can be expressed in many different ways, according to the development of the personality. In the same way, the colors of the chakra, which are expressed in the aura, can change. In the above example, the color of the first, or base, chakra can appear in different shades of red, from dark, "dirty" red, which indicates extreme materialistic behavior, or addiction to drugs or alcohol, to bright, "clean" red, which can be indicative of a sensitive person who copes with his surroundings well, but is mainly interested in materialistic matters.

This situation is likely to be repeated in the other chakras, and of course, will be manifested in the colors of the whole aura. The more a person focuses on one aspect of life and awareness, such as creativity, materialism, mental development, spiritual development, and so on, the more this will be expressed in the activity of the chakra that is responsible for this field. This affects the state of the other chakras too, because of their interrelationship, as well as all the person's fields of awareness and existence, and his conscious bodies. When a strong frequency of a certain color is seen in the aura – yellow, for instance – it shows that most of the person's consciousness is focused on the solar plexus chakra. This may indicate sensitivity in the stomach. It may also indicate much greater concentration on the activities of the third chakra – for example, the desire to be freer or independent and uncommitted. These attempts, which focus on the action of the third chakra, are projected onto the entire aura and make the yellow into the dominant color at that time.

✹ CHAKRAS ✹

The conscious bodies are linked to the aura, to the electromagnetic field, via the chakras. According to the colors of the person's aura, it is possible to know if his awareness is located more in the physical, mental, spiritual, or intellectual layer, and if there is some kind of imbalance between these areas and the action of the chakras.

✺ CHAKRAS ✺

The petals and stems of the chakras

A linking energetic thread of subtle energetic matter flows through the crown chakra and penetrates the physical body. It passes in a straight line from the head to the perineal area (the point that is located between the genitals and the anus). Every chakra has "petals" and a "stem." The stems of the crown and base chakras are open and integral to the central energetic thread. The rest of the chakras are located along this energetic thread. They have petals that open into the anterior part of the aura field, and stems that radiate into the posterior part of the aura field. Most of the stems remain closed, but the petals are flexible, and open and close like the petals of a flower. They move, open, and close according to the various life situations and feelings we experience. When the chakra is flexible, and can open and close like the petals of a flower, it is healthy. This flexibility is not a given. There could be situations in which the flexibility of the chakra is not optimal. It becomes rigid, the energies do not flow properly, and ultimately, the chakra, in such a situation, can become blocked.

Blocked chakras are not rare. These blockages can be caused by various things – generally by long-term processes. A severe or cumulative trauma, too, that affects a particular chakra, is liable to cause it to lose its flexibility or to become blocked relatively quickly. An extreme example of this is a rape, which can seriously affect the sexual chakra. An immediate blockage may occur, and this affects all the areas of the victim's life. There can also be a gradual hardening of the chakra, in which the chakra becomes blocked as a result of the attack. Having said this, except for severe traumas, the process of loss of flexibility of the chakra and its loss of the ability to open and close according to the situations of life is generally gradual and lengthy.

We can compare the action of the healthy chakra to that of a valve. It closes when necessary, and opens as need be. It does not open up to unwanted energy or to a negative reaction, but lets it flow over it without filtering it inside. In contrast, it can open itself up to suitable and correct energy. So it is possible to see the importance not only of the opening of the chakra, but also of its ability to close when necessary.

These marvelous capabilities of the chakras can be disrupted, as we said, by severe traumas, but there are additional factors that affect the chakras: regular use of drugs and medications, excessive intake of alcohol and tobacco, and regular or prolonged use of medical anesthesia. After a local or general anesthetic, the chakras require immediate treatment and balancing.

These situations can cause the chakras to remain open – resulting in the person being extremely vulnerable and sensitive to external influences – or to cause them to harden gradually and close, so that the person loses certain abilities and sensations that derive from the action of a particular chakra.

These situations can be treated by healing and color therapy (to which the chakras respond wonderfully). However, most of the work on the chakras is self-treatment, which includes awareness, visualization – especially of color and movement – and conscious breathing.

Balancing the chakras

As we mentioned previously, our chakras react to color, light, sound, smell, and other energetic frequencies that help bring them into a state of balance, open them, and stimulate their action.

There are many different methods of balancing the chakras. Below, we will suggest a number of methods that have a significant effect and a profound and long-term action.

Balancing by means of color

As we will see later on, each chakra is linked to a color, affected by a color, and contains a certain color. We can say that all of the chakras contain all the shades, but there is a particular color that is dominant, and exerts the main influence on the action of the chakra. When the action of the chakra is not harmonious, we can discern a situation in which the color of the chakra is faded, unclear, "dirty" (that is, its tone is not clear), and so on.

The link between the chakra and the colors that activate, stimulate and balance it is not arbitrary. People who are gifted with the ability to see the aura field and discern its colors as well as the colors of the chakras have investigated and examined the link between the chakras and the colors for thousands of years and have reached conclusions. However, it is not necessary to possess the gift of seeing the colors of the chakras in order to feel how a certain color affects a certain chakra; it is sufficient to experiment and see for yourself the immediate and significant effect of the color of the chakra on the chakra.

As we mentioned previously, the aura is composed of all the colors of the spectrum in different combinations and amounts. The astral body is characterized by an extremely delicate balance of colors, and any state of emotional, physical or spiritual imbalance will be reflected in the appearance of a certain color or colors in a more dominant way among the colors of the aura, or in the blurring or swallowing of other colors. Maintaining the balance in the colors of the aura and mainly in the colors of the ethereal body is essential and vital to the wholeness of every layer of life.

We can easily see how a particular color affects us mentally. When we enter a red room, for instance, we can feel the stimulating effect of the color. We can easily feel the cheerful effect of the color orange, and the palpably calming effect of blue in a place where blue is dominant – such as the beach. So long as the balance between the colors of the aura is maintained, and all the colors of the chakras are clear, balanced and harmonious, the person feels healthy and calm, and his life runs in a smooth, harmonious, and fulfilling manner. When this balance is upset, it can cause various diseases, types of discomfort, unbalanced moods and negative states such as fatigue, nervousness, depression and so on, as well as states of imbalance in various areas of life such as marital relations, work, creativity, and so on.

The lack of balance between the colors of the aura can be protracted and long-term, or temporary, stemming from a specific cause, such as an emotional outburst, a quarrel, an argument, an accident, an illness, and so on. In those situations and following them, until the person liberates himself from the mass of non-positive emotions or from the influence of the lack of physical balance, a state of imbalance in the colors of the aura and the chakras that are involved in the emotional, physical, or spiritual process is liable to occur. Sometimes, this situation can reach the point of a significant weakening of certain colors in the aura, while other colors become dominant and appear in areas of the aura and the chakras that do not support the general balance of the person. In such states, it is important to discover the color or colors that are missing or that are in a state of imbalance, and complete them in one of the ways described in the book.

Projecting colors

Projecting colors is performed by the practitioner after he has made a diagnosis using various methods. However, it is important to mention that the practitioner does not "invent" the facts. He operates according to the information he receives from the patient in various ways. The patient himself can also discover which colors he is lacking. This can be done by intuition – a "gut feeling" about the missing color. We can observe our reactions to the different colors, thereby identifying the color we need, the color we are attracted to, and, in contrast, the color that makes us feel uncomfortable. Sometimes, the colors with which the person does not feel comfortable can be colors he is lacking, or colors with whose energetic action he is not in perfect harmony. In this situation, it is worthwhile checking to see which chakra is linked to this color, to read about the functioning of the chakra carefully, and to identify whether there is a state of imbalance or a blockage in the chakra. People with highly developed visual perception can see the color when they "order" the color they need. Note that the balancing of the third eye chakra and the awareness of its action, will contribute greatly to the person's ability to know the colors necessary for the balance of his chakras and aura colors.

Intuitive discovery of the color

In order to achieve maximal accuracy, this technique should be performed in a state of calmness and alertness and an overall comfortable feeling. You will need about 15 minutes in which you will not be disturbed. Unplug the phone and choose a place to sit or lie down in – wherever you feel comfortable. If you tend to fall asleep easily, it is preferable for you to do this exercise sitting up. Some people do the exercise standing up, but in order to achieve good relaxation and calming of the body, it is better to do it sitting or lying down.

Take several deep, slow, and comfortable breaths and close your eyes. Relax your entire body, starting with your toes, and going up, relaxing and calming every single organ. When you feel relaxed, calm and focused, request – either aloud or mentally – to know what color you need at this moment in order to balance the colors of your aura.

The answer can come in different ways. You may receive clear information about the color you need; you may feel a kind of voice within you telling you what the color is; you may see one or more spots of colors in front of your eyes, or a ray of light in the color you need; you may see the name of the color, or as you open your eyes, you may see a color that you feel is the color you need. As we said, more than one color may appear.

Discovering the color needed by someone else

This technique is used by many practitioners and healers for determining the color the patient needs. It is very similar to the first one, the difference being that now you have to be tuned into and linked up to the patient.

Certain people find it easier to discover the color when the patient is next to them. In such a case, you must stand behind the patient and place your hands on his shoulders, or sit opposite him and gaze into his eyes. Then you must shut your eyes and invite the color needed by the patient to appear in ways similar to those in the basic technique.

However, even when the patient is not in the room, it is possible to perform the technique effectively. In the latter case, it is important to find a point that stimulates a link between you and the patient. This could be his voice, his image in our imagination or in a picture, an object that reminds us of him, and so on. Different people link up more easily via various qualities – such as a picture, voice, contact, and so on, according to the openness of their fine senses (which we will elaborate upon in the chapter dealing with the third eye chakra). After the link has been established, it is possible to receive information, an image or a feeling about the color the person needs for balancing the colors of his aura and chakras. In any event, it is important to be sure that the link to the patient is clear, and the color that appears is the color needed by the patient *and not by the practitioner*. When you want to know the color that is needed, it is important to mention the person's name. You can mention the problem from which he is suffering, and request to know the most suitable color for balancing his problems and his overall state of health in a given time.

Methods of treatment with color

After we have discovered the color needed by us or by the patient, there are many different methods at our disposal for providing the missing color. Of course, in addition to the techniques that were suggested for discovering the color or colors that are not present in the balance or missing in the aura, it is possible to get a reliable picture of the situation by understanding the condition of the different chakras. When we are aware of the fact that a particular chakra is operating below par or unharmoniously, it is possible to use its color. Balancing the color of the chakra will affect the balance of all the colors of the aura simultaneously. In the above mentioned techniques, we wanted to know the color that was **missing** in the colors of the aura or in the particular chakra. To the same extent, we can ask if a particular color is in a state of imbalance or excess. When a particular color is dominant as a result of a certain chakra's imbalanced action with a tendency toward hyperactivity, we use its complementary color in order to balance the condition.

Every color has a complementary color. In many cases, an imbalance in the basic color of one of the chakras is liable to create an imbalance in its complementary color as well. It is very important to be familiar with the complementary colors, since during color projection, too, it is important to project the missing basic color as well as its complementary color in order to create perfect balance. In addition, the projection of certain colors can exert a very powerful effect. Red and blue tend to be intense in their action during projection and afterwards. Red is liable to cause overstimulation and sometimes a slight feeling of agitation, even if we have discovered that that is the missing color needed for creating balance, while blue can cause a feeling of heaviness, fatigue, and sometimes a mild drop in mood. When projecting those colors, we must always make sure to project their complementary colors as well.

The complementary color of red is turquoise. The complementary color of green is magenta. The complementary color of blue is orange. The complementary color of purple is yellow. The complementary color of indigo is gold – and the opposite.

Methods of projecting colors

Color projection is the most common method used in color therapy. It is possible to project color in several ways:

Focusing on color cards: Color cards are cards that can be made at home. Cut stiff cardboard or white construction paper into a card the size of a playing-card. Then paint it in a clear and vivid shade of the color. If you saw the color during meditation for discovering the required color, it is advisable to choose the same color you saw while meditating. You can also make a card in the complementary color. Look at the clock before starting, and then gaze at the color card for a few minutes, when you are calm, your body is relaxed, and you feel an overall serenity and a slightly meditative feeling. The moment you feel replete, put down the card and look at the clock to see how long you spent looking at the basic color. Now spend a third of that time gazing at the complementary color. Some people only look at the card for a few moments, and then close their eyes and see the color in their mind's eye. This method is also very effective.

Colored light bulbs: In color therapy, many practitioners use colored light bulbs or light bulbs wrapped in colored cellophane paper. The colored light is projected onto the patient, who is sitting at some distance from it (making sure that the light does not dazzle him), or is projected from behind the patient. Generally speaking, a basic color is projected here too, and a third of the time is spent projecting its complementary color in order to maintain the balance. Projecting the complementary color is also good in cases in which there is a fear of an inaccurate projection of the color, that is, uncertainty regarding the amount of time the color should be projected, which can create an excess of the basic color. In such situations, projecting the complementary color restores the balance.

✿ CHAKRAS ✿

Colored clothing: Various colored clothes have a significant effect on the person's mental feeling, and, by choosing the color of the clothing, it is possible to help balance the missing color. This is a very simple method, and is highly recommended for self-treatment. Some people use it mainly when the color imbalance occurs in the mental and emotional layer.

Eating food in the missing color: Eating foods of various colors also has an effect on the balance of the colors. Of course, we are not referring to foods that are dyed with food coloring, but rather to foods whose natural coloring corresponds with our need for a particular color – for instance, red for balancing the base chakra: tomatoes, red bell peppers, and so on; orange for balancing the sex chakra: carrots, yams, pumpkin, and so on. There are practitioners who are in the habit of recommending balancing color by means of foods, especially when the imbalance is reflected in the patient's physical state.

Balancing colors by means of precious stones and crystals: Precious stones and crystals occur in a tremendous range of colors and shades. Besides the color of the stone, every mineral possesses unique, powerful and extraordinary properties, with a significant action on the entire human organism in general and on the electromagnetic field in particular. When you know what color you need, you can find a suitable stone, even without any prior knowledge of its properties and qualities. All you have to do is go to one of the crystal stores and look at stones in the color you need. Concentrate on and tune into your objective – finding a stone that will help you complete the missing color/s in your aura or in a particular chakra, for the sake of your general balance in all layers. Select and purchase the stone to which you feel greatly attracted. This is the simplest and most effective method, since stones have the ability to link up to us, and we can pick up which stone suits us intuitively, without conscious thought. (Of course, we can use the stones that are suggested for balancing each of the chakras, in accordance with their additional properties other than their color suitability, but it is still important to check whether you link up well to the particular stone.) If you intuitively picked a stone in a suitable color, it is almost certain that after you ask the salesperson its name, take an interest in it and examine it, you will discover how suitable it is for you. After purchasing the stone, it is important to find you if it can be purified in salt water and how it should be treated and looked after. (Do not cleanse it without checking first, since there are stones that are destroyed when they come into contact with salt, or are sensitive to water.) Soak it in water mixed with sea salt for three hours. Then place it on the windowsill for 24 hours. You must not use the stone without purifying it! One of the properties of stones is absorbing energies, and you do not want to take over the energies of all the people who felt the stone, quarried it and traded it. After purification, you can use the stone in any way you want. You can hold it in your hand, carry it in your pocket, place it on the relevant chakra, meditate with it, place it on any organ you feel a need to place it on, wear it, or simply gaze at it. Even gazing at the stone for a few moments can help balance the missing or unbalanced color. After using the stone, it must be purified under cold running water for three to five minutes, and placed in sunlight or moonlight, since it absorbs some of the non-positive energies and projects its energies onto you. For that reason, it requires reinforcing and refreshing. It is necessary to relate to crystals respectfully and gratefully, as you relate to your physician, your holistic healer, or your teacher.

Colored ray of light: This is one of the most common ways of projecting color in healing, and its effect is very powerful. The method can be used for self-treatment as well as for treating others. After you find out what color is required in order to balance and reinforce the aura or chakra (your own or your patient's), imagine a ray of light in the requisite color coming down from above. If you do not perform this technique as a continuation of the technique of discovering the color, which includes relaxation and entering a meditative state, you will have to relax your body and take conscious breaths until you feel serene and calm and ready to receive the color. Now, imagine in your mind's eye the ray of light descending from above, penetrating your head, filling your body and all your organs with color, continuing to fill your body with every breath while going down your spine, flowing downward and going out through your feet into the bowels of the earth. You can see the ray of light projected onto the patient for 15-20 minutes or according to your intuitive feeling even without imagining the process of filling up with color. It is possible, and sometimes important, to project the complementary color onto him as well for a third of the time in order to maintain balance. The power of the treatment with color projection is enormous.

Projecting via the hands: This is a very powerful technique that is mainly recommended for treatment. It is best applied by people who are already experienced in healing, Reiki (mainly), or other healing techniques. People who are unable to empty themselves of self-related thoughts and emotions should not apply it. The treatment can be performed on the person himself, in his presence, but also when he is not physically present in the room.

Initially, you will have to find out what color the person needs. Experienced practitioners can sense the color right at the beginning of the projection, and it is possible that even without much experience, but with developed intuition, you will discover a similar sensation. When the person is present in the room, perform the projection in one of the following ways:

* Ask the person to lie down, instruct him to perform the relaxation process, which includes deep breathing and relaxing his organs, and perform the projection standing beside him, your hands over his body, at a distance you feel to be suitable.

* Ask the person to sit, instruct him to perform the relaxation process, and sit opposite him, holding your hands spread out toward him.

* Ask the person to sit, instruct him to perform the relaxation process, and stand or sit behind him with your hands spread out toward him.

If you intend to treat a person who is not in the room, you will have to imagine his image in your mind's eye, sitting or lying in front of you, and perform the projection with your hands exactly as if he were next to you physically. You can also use visualization of the person's name, preferably in block capitals. Although ostensibly the spread hands project the color into the whole room, they are aimed at and reach the person on whose name you are concentrating.

And now for the projection process itself: Empty yourself of every self-related thought and emotion and fill up with energy. You can imagine a golden or white light descending from above, penetrating your head, and filling your whole body until it envelops and protects it with its light.

Now ask for the color the person needs, or, if you know it, think of it or see it in your mind's eye.

Calm, serene, and focused, turn your hands to the patient and begin to project the color onto him, imagining in your mind's eye how the color is filling him or the chakra to which you are projecting the color, releasing blockages, healing, balancing, and stimulating vitality.

You can project the basic color for 15 minutes, and then project the complementary color for five minutes in order to maintain the balance of the colors.

A colored ellipse of light: This technique is very similar to the previous color projection techniques, except that here, instead of seeing a spot of color or a ray of colored light, you see yourself or your patient surrounded by a large and shining ellipse of the appropriate color. The ellipse protects and guards you or your patient from unwanted influences, preserves the self-energies, opens blockages, and protects and improves health in all layers.

It is important to mention that black is not used in color therapy and healing! It is neither projected nor sent. Sometimes, it is used in clothing in order to give a feeling of protection, but it is not used in the healing techniques. White, because of its cleanness and purity, is thought to be difficult to project, since it is not always easy to ensure that it is projected clean and pure, and for this reason is not recommended.

In contrast to black and white, gold is good and suitable in every color projection and color healing, since it is the universal and sublime healing color. Green is suitable for treatment and projection in every defective physical state and for every health problem except tumors.

Using aromatic oils and incense from medicinal herbs to balance the chakras

Aromatic oils have a far-reaching effect on the actions of the various bodily systems, on the emotional state, and on the spiritual state. These oils, like the incense that is produced from different plants, have been used for such purposes for thousands of years, and have been recognized as exerting a profound effect on the spiritual layer. In various cultures, incense and aromatic oils that were produced by various manual methods were used to help people enter states of meditation and trance, to stimulate the spiritual layers, to exorcise demons, to perform various rituals, and so on.

The most common uses of aromatic oils are for balancing mental, spiritual and physical states, for healing various physical problems, for preventing diseases, and for purifying the body, mind, spirit, and home. The aromatic oils can cause a clear feeling of stimulation, and, on the other hand, engender a calming feeling. The fragrances of the flowers and plants, which absorb vitalizing energy from the earth and from the light, affect our soul and link up to us energetically in a perfect manner. Of all the senses, the sense of smell has the most rapid effect on our brains. It reaches the subconscious knowledge stored in our brains directly. As an example of this, we can see the way in which certain odors immediately evoke memories that are connected to the odor. These can even be memories whose origins lie in the first years of childhood. The action of the aromatic oils, which contain an extremely concentrated essence of the fragrance of the plant, touch our soul and our spirit deeply, to the point of removing emotional and spiritual blockages and stimulating inner knowledge and recognition, while promoting the development of supportive spiritual processes. This influence is known for the way in which the chakras respond to the energetic action of the aromatic essences.

In the chapters that deal with the various chakras, the oils that are known to exert especially powerful effects on each of the chakras are mentioned. Some oils cause the chakra to be stimulated, while others calm, balance or purify their action. You can also sense for yourself, by smelling the aromatic essences of the different oils, how they affect the action of your chakras, and to which of the chakras they are connected very strongly for you personally.

There are several treatment methods for balancing the chakras using aromatic oils. It must be remembered that the essential oils, with the exception of lavender, have a relatively high level of toxicity. For this reason, they must not be applied to the body in their undiluted form, and must be mixed with carrier oils. Carrier oils are also produced from various plants. Some of the most widely used carrier oils are peanut oil, almond oil, apricot kernel oil, and grape seed oil. Of course, there are other types of carrier oils that are suitable for different purposes and skin types.

Essential oil burner: The first method for balancing the chakras using aromatic oils employs the steam that rises from oil that is heated by a candle in an essential oil burner. The essential oil burner is generally made of porcelain (this is the most recommended kind). Its upper part contains a saucer, either separate from the rest of the utensil or joined to it, in which water (preferably mineral water) is placed. The oils are dripped into the water. In the lower part of the burner, there is an opening for placing a small candle. (The candles used in burners are small and round, usually in little aluminum holders that prevent the burner from being spattered with wax. They are sometimes called "tea candles.") Eight to twelve drops of oil are added to the water in the burner, according to the size of the room. It is possible to use a few drops of several different kinds of oil, but no more than four kinds should be used. The candle is lit, and it heats up the saucer containing the water. Within a few minutes, the steam from the oil begins to rise and spread through the room. In addition to its balancing effect on the action of the chakra for which the aromatic oil is suitable, its effect on the mental layer is rapid and easily felt, and the use of a burner is suitable for the general purification of the room, for helping the person enter a meditative state and for opening the respiratory tract.

The choice of balancing the chakras by means of aromatic oils in a burner is particularly suitable when we are focusing on treating the mental aspect – conditions of tension and stress, nervousness, bad moods, fatigue, exhaustion, memory problems, studying for exams – and for stimulation and concentration, solving sexual problems that stem from an emotional source, and so on.

(When using a burner, pay attention to several "heavier" oils that do not float on the surface of the water, but rather sink beneath it. When using clove or benzoin oil, for instance, and in many cases when using sandalwood oil, it is advisable to drip the oil onto the side of the saucer, above the water line, in order to prevent the oil from sinking to the bottom. Another important point is that when we purchase a burner, we must under no circumstances purchase one made of metal, or whose saucer is made of metal. While this kind of burner is still sold in New Age stores, metal reacts with the aromatic blend with blatantly unhealthy implications. After use, it is extremely important to clean the burner with warm water and dishwashing detergent, and sometimes let it soak in a little hot water and rub the saucer with half a lemon in order to remove the stains produced by the oils we have used lately. This problem occurs mainly when using a burner made of clay that has been glazed with a substance of some kind, and allowing the candle to burn even after the water has evaporated almost completely. In such cases, an accumulation of oil residues builds up, which is liable to jeopardize the action of the oils placed in the burner. It is no less important to mention that various synthetic blends are sold in weird and wonderful fragrances; these are sometimes labeled "for use in a burner," "oil for meditation," and so on. These blends are not suitable for treatment under any circumstances, and do not have the same effect on the chakras as the pure oils. These oils must not be spread on the skin, and it is not even advisable to use them in a burner. It is important to make sure that the oil is authentic by purchasing it in a reputable store or in a drugstore where the salesperson can attest to the fact that it is pure oil. The mixture of pure oil with synthetic oil undermines the action of the pure oil.)

Massage: Massage is a common and popular way of getting the aromatic oils to penetrate the body via the skin. The massage is performed with a carrier oil, and it has many advantages, both in and of itself and in conjunction with aromatherapy. Massage combines touch, which itself is therapeutic – both physically and mentally – with the action of the oils. The penetration of the oils makes the massage effective, and the massage itself ensures a better penetration of the oils into the skin. In addition, massage stimulates the blood and lymph flow and the circulatory system, activates and invigorates the immune system, and in this way stimulates all of the body's systems. Massage helps cleanse the body of waste and toxins, and causes an improvement in the excretion of waste from the body. In cases of pain, especially muscular pains, the relief attained by means of massage with aromatic oils is extremely significant, and this is also true for conditions that require the reduction of swelling and congestion. Massage causes a feeling of general calm and repose, in accordance with the use of oils, and on the other hand can help the person feel more alert and energetic. On the mental plane, massage helps open energetic blockages, reduce mental tension, release mental reactions, and raise the level of energy and vitality.

In order to stimulate the chakras, it is possible to gently massage the areas in which the chakras are situated, using suitable aromatic oils. The massage is highly recommended for release and relief in cases of tension in the spine (by means of neuromuscular work, i.e., work on the nerves that branch off the spinal cord into the body), since it achieves excellent results. The release of tension helps bring about a better flow of energy, and contributes to the balancing and opening of all the chakras.

Spreading the oils: Spreading the oils is performed in a similar manner to massage, with one important difference: the oil is spread onto the skin gently, and is not massaged into it with massage movements. The spreading can be performed on small infants, elderly people, people whose level of vitality is low, and in cases in which treatment must not be administered in the form of massage. Reasons for this are: debility, ongoing treatment with medications, high blood pressure, being in a post-operative state, or an acute phase of a disease.

We spread the oil on the chakra region in circular movements. We select an oil that is suitable for the chakra, and pay attention to the direction of the spreading: to open the chakra, we spread the oil in a circular, clockwise direction. To close the chakra, when it is overactive (in fact, actual closing does not occur, but the excessive activity is balanced), we make circular, anti-clockwise movements. For balance, we make circular movements in both clockwise and anti-clockwise directions, alternately, several times, for five to ten minutes.

The spreading itself is a fast and easy way of linking up to the chakras. Since the chakras are energy centers, the very fact of thinking about them and touching them affects their action. Therefore, while spreading the oils, it is advisable to direct one's thoughts to stimulating/balancing/opening/cleaning the chakra. When in addition to the spreading and the thought we also imagine the color of the chakra, the effect is reinforced.

Baths: Treatment with aromatic oils in baths is wonderful for treating skin problems and improving the appearance of the skin and its vitality, for relieving pain, for lowering a fever (not in conditions that require medical care, however), for physical and mental relaxation, and for treating a broad range of emotional problems. Taking a bath with aromatic oils creates a calming and enjoyable sensation, and is also recommended for people who are not suffering from any kind of problem for relaxation, relieving tension and treating the skin. Taking a bath with oils for balancing and opening certain chakras can be a marvelous experience. The bath is especially recommended when we want to balance and open the sex chakra, and, in parallel, we identify an emotional imbalance and a certain imbalance in accepting sexuality. The combination of water, the naked body – which arouses in us a fiercer desire to accept it – and the aromatic oils is a highly effective opening and stimulating process for all four lower chakras, and for this reason also makes the opening of the upper chakras possible. Taking a bath with aromatic oils is highly recommended in cases in which the person feels somewhat uncomfortable about his body. This feeling can occur during the bath, so that we can be aware of it, notice which organs it focuses on, and begin a process of accepting these organs and balancing the chakra to which they are connected.

When balancing the chakras by using aromatic oils in a bath, it is important to adhere to several rules: The actual washing (with soap, etc.) must be done beforehand, since after the aromatic bath, we do not soap ourselves or even rinse ourselves off. We leave the oils that were mixed into the bath-water on our skin and so as not to jeopardize their action. We should not dry ourselves off vigorously, but simply wrap ourselves in a towel and go and rest. The rest after the bath with aromatic oils is very important for the continued action of the oils on the body and on the energetic layer, and for this reason it is advisable to take the bath before going to sleep. In any event, at least an hour of rest after the bath is essential for lengthening the process of the action of the oils on the chakras.

After adding 7-8 drops of aromatic oil to the bath-water, the recommended length of time for soaking in the bath is between 15 and 20 minutes. In order to balance the chakras, we can use oils for each chakra, choosing four oils that *together* treat all the chakras. As we will see, several oils are suitable for treating more than one or two chakras.

Using crystals to balance the chakras

Crystals are highly powerful tools for stimulating awareness. They can be used in many meditations, and they are among the simplest and most excellent tools that exist for balancing the chakras, the energetic bodies, and the various layers of the universe. The broad range of colors of the crystals, as well as their multifarious properties, makes them into a powerful tool for opening, cleansing, and balancing the chakras, and their action is palpable and fast.

The frequencies of light, color, and sound, as well as the unique frequencies of minerals exert a powerful and significant effect on the frequencies that surround and activate the human body. It would be easier for us to understand this supposition if we could visualize the movement of atoms. The atoms that comprise the world of matter, which is ostensibly solid and stable, are in a perpetual state of vibration. Although the naked eye cannot discern these vibrations, they are nevertheless constantly present.

When the energies of the crystals are "added" to those of human beings, a combination of a new vibrational force is created.

The combination between human energies and mineral energies causes the person to rise to a higher and more open state of awareness. When the mineral performs its function and its vocation when we link our energies to its energies, we gain additional knowledge and understanding of our physical, emotional and spiritual state. The frequencies of the various crystals work in a balancing and cleansing manner on the frequencies of our physical body, as well as on the frequencies of the energetic bodies – from the ethereal body, the emotional body, the mental body and the spiritual (intuitive) body to the karmic body.

Using crystals to balance the chakras can be done at any time and in any situation, even without concentrating consciously on the process!

Carrying the stone in a pocket, or even wearing it, will profoundly affect the state of the chakra to which it is linked, as well as the frequencies of all the bodies.

There are many ways to use crystals for balancing the chakras:

Placing crystals: Placing crystals on the chakra in order to stimulate/open/purify/ balance it is one of the most popular ways of balancing the chakras. It is possible to place one suitable stone on one of the chakras. However, placing a crystal set consisting of several stones on several chakras at the same time helps not only to balance and open the chakras, but also to join them up and link them, reinforce the flow between them, and create an overall harmonious action of several chakras together. The crystal set, in which suitable crystals are placed on each of the chakras, is one of the most powerful ways of balancing all the chakras and of creating harmony in their action, at the same time opening blockages not only in the chakras themselves, but also between them.

Wearing and carrying crystals: Wearing a crystal on various parts of the body affects the action of the chakra even when we do not focus our awareness on balancing it. The side we choose to carry or wear the stone is important – the right side or the left side of the body. The left side of the body is the receiving side, which is more sensitive, and tends to receive the energies directed at it more quickly. Wearing a crystal on the organs of the left side of the body is effective for controlling and neutralizing external energies (especially when the stones in question have protective properties). The right side is the "giving," projecting side. Wearing stones on the organs of the right side of the body intensifies our abilities, the projecting ability of our personality, our actions and our productivity.

We can wear the stones in different ways, each one with its own uniqueness and action. While wearing the stone in a ring does not concentrate on any particular chakra, it enables us to gaze at the stone that is set in a ring and link up to it. This linking up creates an immediate reaction in the chakra to which the stone is linked. Wearing the stone as a ring is recommended when the person discovers that linking up with the stone by gazing at it has a profound effect on him and serves as a powerful way for him to link up with the stones (certain people feel a stronger link by gazing, while others prefer to hold or place them on different parts of their body), and he is interested in working on opening and balancing one of the chakras every day. A ring that contains the stone that helps balance the particular chakra will help the person be conscious of being attuned to balancing the particular chakra during the entire day, and will help with in-depth but gradual work in opening and balancing the chakra. Certain insights may arise in this process as a result of the opening and balancing of the chakra.

Wearing a stone in the region of the neck and below it, in the region of the hollow of the clavicle, is an excellent way of balancing, opening and cleansing the throat chakra. Every stone worn in this region affects the functions of the throat chakra. Necklaces and strings of beads that are worn in the neck region affect the throat chakra and the abilities to communicate and express oneself, both alone and with others.

Wearing pendants is an excellent way of balancing and opening the heart and solar plexus chakras. The stone must be matched to the chakra, and so must the length of the chain of the pendant. Carrying the stone in the shirt pocket also affects the action of the heart chakra.

Stones that are set in barrettes and tiaras affect the crown chakra. It is possible to use them for stimulating the action of the chakra, but with great caution. First of all, it is not advisable to place the barrette with the stone on the head for any length of time, but rather for a period of no longer than a half-hour to an hour. Second, it is importance to ensure that the stone chosen is suitable for the chakra. For instance, stones that are suitable for the base chakra, as well as more "earthy" stones, are not suitable for the crown chakra. In contrast, certain stones, which help open the crown chakra and the third eye chakra can cause us to "float" if we wear them as barrettes or tiaras, and can disrupt our everyday functioning. The stones that may be suitable are smoky quarts, sodalite, amethyst, sapphire, zircon and emerald. Zircons are especially suitable for preparing tiaras. In any case, a stone must not be set in a barrette, nor must a barrette with a stone be purchased before checking carefully and concentrating fully on what sensation the stone causes. An unsuitable stone is liable to cause dizziness or unpleasant sensations. The stones that are suitable for setting in barrettes and tiaras are mainly stones that contribute to personal development and spiritual growth, but do not cause significant floating.

Belts set with stones and minerals affect the sex chakra and our level of vitality. Orange stones, such as garnet or carnelian, in a belt that is worn relatively low, can be suitable. Belts set with turquoise can give an energetic or calming feeling. Carnelian helps raise motivation when it is worn in the hip region, agate increases energy, and jasper help achieve a feeling of balance.

Carrying the stone in a pocket also exerts an effect on the chakras. As we said before, carrying stones in a shirt pocket affects the heart chakra, while carrying stones in pants pockets has a certain effect on the sex chakra.

For grounding, when the base chakra is not working to full capacity and the person feels uprooted and floating, it is advisable to wear ankle bracelets with grounding base chakra stones such as hematite or jasper.

Crystal gazing: Crystal gazing is meditation, even if this is not the person's intention. The moment we link up to the crystal, even by looking at it, we link up to its frequencies. Crystal gazing affects one of the chakras, and has a tangible effect on the chakra itself. We use this technique in several of the crystal meditations.

Crystal sets: By means of sets of crystals, we balance all the chakras, open them, and cleanse them. Below there are some recommended crystal sets, but it is important to mention that when working with crystals, our intuition and personal feeling are among the most important tools. We must rely on our feelings toward the stones, choose the ones that are suitable for us and see how they affect us personally before we choose them for use in a set for balancing the chakras. Moreover, we must be aware of changes in the length of time of the crystal set, since it can become shorter or longer according to the person's feeling.

Crystal sets for balancing the chakras

In the chapters that describe the action of the chakras, you will find a list of the crystals and stones that are suitable for each chakra. Choose one suitable stone for each of the chakras. Carefully cleanse the seven stones you have chosen before using them. They can be purified in a bowl of water with salt (except for fluorite and pyrite) for about three hours, and afterwards rinsed well in water from the faucet.

After purifying the seven stones, take the first stone – the one that is suitable for the base chakra. Hold it in your hand, and direct your thoughts to stimulating the power of the stone to open, balance, stimulate and cleanse the base chakra. You can even "speak" to it and tell it, "I have chosen you to balance, open and cleanse my base chakra." Our words and thoughts have an obvious energetic effect on the stones, and they strengthen their natural action and match their frequencies to ours. Do the same with all of the stones. If you want to use a crystal set for treating someone else, mention the person's name, or see him in your mind's eye while you are programming each of the stones for balancing and opening the chakras. This is a very simple crystal set both for self-treatment and for treating others.

The crystal set is applied lying down. It is advisable to change the sheets before commencing, or to spread a clean sheet over a thin mattress on the floor or on the treatment table. It is a good idea to take a shower before beginning the treatment (self-treatment, too), and to drink a glass of water. The set should not be applied after a heavy meal (or on an empty stomach, when you feel hungry; the best is after a light meal).

Place the stones you have chosen on a clean piece of fabric or a towel on a low table or stool next to you, or on the floor if you intend to lie on a mattress or mat on the floor. Place a medium-size bowl one-third filled with water nearby. The bowl must be large enough to contain and cover all the stones without the water overflowing as a result of the volume of the stones. (You can check this beforehand, prior to programming the stones to balance the chakras.)

Lie on your back and begin to take deep, slow breaths. Relax all the muscles of your body, starting with the muscles in your toes, and go upward, relaxing each muscle, including your facial muscles. The recommended way for achieving deep physical relaxation is to contract each muscle tightly and relax it quickly. When you feel relaxed, calm, and comfortable, place the stone you have chosen for balancing the base chakra on the chakra. Concentrate on the feeling for a few minutes while you listen to the rhythm of your breathing. Take the second stone, which is suitable for the sex chakra, place it on the chakra, and concentrate on the feeling for a few minutes, breathing consciously. Continue in this way until you have placed all seven stones on the appropriate chakras. During the entire process, make sure to take deep, slow abdominal breaths. Close your eyes and let all thoughts pass through your head without relating to them. Just let them go by without taking any notice of them. Concentrate on breathing, and feel the pleasant vibrations and the warming and healing sensation the stones transmit to your body. At a certain point, you may feel a need to take off one of the stones, or one of them will fall off by itself. This is a natural occurrence, because it is certainly possible that each of the chakras is in a different state of openness and balance than the others and reacts differently to the stone placed on it. Thus, there could be chakras that require a shorter length of time for balancing. Remain like this for 10-20 minutes. You will be able to sense intuitively when to stop and remove the stones. Now, start to remove the stones one by one. Begin with the crown chakra, and continue chakra by chakra, until you finally remove the stone from the base chakra. Place each stone in the bowl of water (place it in such a way that it will not overflow onto the bed or floor, and does not require you to make any movement that is so big that you will drop the rest of the stones). When you put the stones in the bowl, dip your fingertips in the water, your intention being to get rid of the unwanted energies that were absorbed in the stone. If for some reason you cannot place a bowl of water beside you, place the stones on the towel or piece of fabric next to you and place them in the bowl later, dipping your fingertips in the water. You can continue resting for a while after removing the stones, letting the pleasant resonance continue enveloping you in its warm light.

A crystal set with generators

A generator is a quartz crystal formation with six facets joined together to form a point. The generator has many different uses in healing, energetic purification, and stimulating energy, and it is used for stimulating other crystals when administering treatment with crystals and crystal sets.

For this crystal set, you will need two generators – a transparent quartz generator, and a medium-size smoky quartz generator. If you do not possess a smoky quartz generator, you can substitute another quartz generator. Moreover, you will need seven stones (as previously), one for each chakra. Go over the list of stones that are suitable for each chakra, and choose the crystals that are most suitable for you. If you possess a crystal that is suitable for one of the chakras, and you feel an affinity for it, use it even if it does not appear on the list.

Perform the crystal set in a quiet, clean and calm room. Light an essential oil burner containing jasmine, frankincense or lavender oil. Place a bowl that is one-third filled with water near you, in which you can place the stones after you have finished using them.

Put a comfortable pillow beneath your head or neck, and lie on your back. Place the smoky quartz crystal under your legs, at a distance of up to 15 centimeters from your feet, with its point facing outward. Place the quartz generator at a distance of five to ten centimeters above your head, with its point facing your head. Relax your whole body, close your eyes, and begin to concentrate on calm and steady breathing. Be conscious of your breathing. When inhaling, feel yourself making the inhaled air flow to every organ in your body. Begin from your feet, and go upward, while filling every single organ with air, healing and soothing it.

After you feel that you are in a calm and comfortable meditative state, see a golden light emanating from the quartz generator above your head and going down your spine, penetrating each of your chakras, filling your entire body with light, and going out of your feet.

Take the stone that is suitable for the base chakra and place it on the chakra. Feel how red light, clear and glowing, is emitted from the stone into your base chakra. See the light warming the chakra, stimulating it to action. Concentrate on this feeling for a few moments.

Take the stone that is suitable for balancing the sex chakra and place it on the chakra. See orange light flowing from the stone into the chakra, enveloping it, stimulating and balancing it. Concentrate on this feeling until you feel replete.

Take the stone that is suitable for the solar plexus chakra and place it on the chakra. See yellow light enveloping the region of the diaphragm, flowing from the stone to the chakra, opening and balancing it. Breathe the yellow light, and continue to make it flow to the chakra in your mind's eye until you feel ready to move on to the next chakra.

Take the stone that is suitable for the heart chakra and place it on the chakra. If you place a pink stone on the chakra, see pink light in your mind's eye flowing from it into the chakra. If you chose a suitable green stone, see green light flowing and filtering into it, activating and balancing it. Concentrate for a few minutes on the feeling of warmth and openness that is awakening in you with the projection of the colors of the chakra.

Take the stone that is suitable for the throat chakra and place it on the chakra. See a blue light flowing from the stone to the region of the throat, filling the chakra, balancing it, cleansing it and opening it, cool and pleasant like pure water. Concentrate on the feeling for a few moments.

Take the stone that is suitable for the third eye chakra and place it on the chakra. See purple or indigo light flowing from the stone into the chakra. Imagine the sight of your cerebral hemispheres, right and left, and see the purple light enveloping them. If you discern black or grayish spots, imagine the purple light filling them, until the two hemispheres are completely enveloped in purple light, and their color is white or purple. Concentrate on the point between your eyebrows and feel the stimulation of the third eye chakra.

Take the stone you have chosen for the crown chakra and place it below the generator quartz (between the generator and your head). Now concentrate on the generator quartz above your head. Breathe deeply and feel the vibrations that are coming to you from the generator quartz and through the stone you have chosen for the crown chakra. Concentrate on breathing and see golden or pink light penetrating from above through the crown chakra, descending along the spine, filling your entire body with light, and continuing through your feet into the bowels of the earth.

Continue lying down for a few minutes, concentrating on the different feelings that are arising in you, and on the frequencies and vibrations that the crystals are transmitting to the various chakras. When you feel ready, start removing the crystals. Remove the generator quartz that is lying above the crown chakra and place it in the bowl of water. Remove the crystal you chose for the crown chakra, and then remove the crystal that you placed on the third eye chakra. Continue removing all the crystals in descending order and placing them in the bowl of water, ending with the smoky quartz generator.

Keep on lying down for a few minutes, and when you feel ready, get up slowly, without any abrupt movements, so that you will not feel dizzy. If you feel as if you are "floating," gently move your leg and arm joints in circular movements, gently stretch a few times, twist your arms and skip lightly several times. Drinking a glass of water after the process is essential. If you still feel dizzy, eat something light.

Using sound and music to balance the chakras

We live in a world that is full of sound (audio) frequencies, but we are not aware of most of them. We do not listen to some of them, while our sense of hearing is not sufficiently sharp to pick up others. In fact, science today is discovering what was known to mystics in ancient times: all the particles in the universe, all the different forms of radiation and of natural forces, are affected by musical structures. The protons and neutrons of different atoms have different musical resonances. When scientists succeeded in identifying the different sounds that express the growth of grass, or the movement of the planets or the clouds, it was found that these sounds are very similar to known musical scales. Actually, the music we listen to today, which is produced by human beings, is an imitation of those natural resonances. Music is live energy with an effect and an ability to penetrate every from of being in the universe, and this accounts for its tremendous effect on the human mind, body, and soul, and its ability to preserve and renew life. Not for nothing did various mystical and religious rituals throughout the world and throughout the ages make extensive use of music and sound. Through music, we can feel unity with the creative force and balance our energies with those of the universe.

However, not all types of music are suitable for this purpose. Various sounds, as well as various musical combinations, evoke a broad range of sensations in us, which exert a different effect on our energetic balance. Certain sounds can upset our balance or inspire fear, aggressiveness, anger, agitation, or panic in us. Other sounds can give us a feeling of tranquillity and calmness, and yet others cause a feeling of elation and spiritual openness. It is not only human beings that are affected by these frequencies, but also animals and plants. Experiments that were conducted by playing different types of music to animals and plants revealed that these living beings have various "musical preferences," and certain music affects them positively, both on the physical and the mental level. (These experiments revealed over and over again that classical music tends to increase growth, crops, and yield both in plants and animals such as hens and milking cows, while rock music tends to disrupt these parameters; popular music generally did not cause any change in either the control or the experimental group.) Just as music affects animals and plants, so it affects human beings, and for this reason it is necessary to pay attention when choosing the music we listen to.

Because the chakras are very powerful energy centers that transform the energy of the universe into the delicate bodies, the aura, and the body's systems, the effect of music on the chakras is enormous. Each chakra has different music that is suitable for stimulating, balancing or calming it. Despite the recommendations given in these chapters, it is important to take into account the fact that when it is a matter of individuals, the different manifestations may change slightly from person to person. The best way to know how a certain type of music affects one of our chakras is to concentrate on the action of the chakra while we are listening, and to feel how the music affects the chakra. (At the end of each chapter dealing with one of the chakras, there is an exercise for linking up to the chakra. You can use the exercise for identifying the effect of the different types of music on the particular chakra.)

When we use different types of music for stimulating, balancing, opening and calming the chakras, it is important to listen to the music calmly and with absolute concentration. It is recommended that we do this lying down or sitting comfortably with a straight back and relaxed limbs. In order to balance the chakras by means of sound and music therapy, it is not enough just to hear the music, but rather to listen to it consciously. We have to put all thoughts, expectations, vexations and inner noise aside and link up to the music. For this reason, when we are administering treatment and using music therapy to balance the chakras, it is important to choose music that is suitable for balancing the chakra, but it is no less important for the patient to be able to link up to this type of music. The objective is to link up to the music until there is a feeling of unity with it, "going into" it and flowing with it, letting it lead us without inhibitions and letting it envelop us with its sounds. As we said before, while listening to music, we have to concentrate on the chakra. It is possible to imagine the musical frequencies flowing to the chakra, enveloping it, balancing, stimulating or soothing it. When suitable music is chosen and listened to with concentration, various images, sensations, visions, emotions, and thoughts could arise. It is not advisable to devote time to them while listening (but rather to focus on the chakra itself), but to remember them and write them down in a notebook dedicated to work on the chakras. Afterwards, it is possible to go through the notes and analyze the sensations that arose during the meditative state of listening while concentrating on the chakra. Sometimes, these images and sensations can tell us about the state of our chakras, indicate the roots of blockages, or reveal various triggers that lead to the creation of imbalances in the chakras.

Using the sensation of nature to balance and open the chakras

We human beings are part of the nature surrounding us. Our immortal souls are not dependent on time or place, and do not operate according to the laws of physics to which our bodies are subjected. Although they "reside" in a physical body, the souls are aware that they are an inseparable part of the whole universe. Our souls relate to nature, to the earth, to animals and to plants as sister souls, as an inseparable part of their being. For the soul, no such human belief as "a superior race" exists, and it does not make any distinction between one person and another, between female and male, between a human being and an animal, and between a human being and a tree. For the soul, they are all equal, and all have one source and one brotherhood.

Our physical body needs the earth for its vitality, and our soul derives life force from the sights and sensation of nature. Over a period of thousands of years, the human race created a lie in its mind, when it tried to view itself as separate from the earth, as not linked to it. We need the trees, the sea, the earth and the animals just as we need air to breathe, and this distance causes man's mind and soul a great deal of suffering, even if it is unconscious. A lack of this awareness stems from man's distancing himself from his soul; it stems from his inability to feel the soul within him and its ways. Just as "in the heights, so it is in the depths," that is, just as it is in the metaphysical layer – the world of the souls, so it is in the material world. The distance from nature, which causes man's distance from his own soul, also causes a broad range of physical problems. Unfortunately, this is a vicious circle. Man detaches himself from the source – which is realized in the most perfect form in nature, becomes unaware of his existence as a soul, harms nature, Mother Earth and her children, the members of the animal and plant kingdoms, and ultimately finds himself at the center of asphalt forests that upset his balance.

Being in nature, the contact with it, feeling, smelling, tasting and observing it, are food for the mind and soul. Sometimes, when he is in a place in which nature expresses itself freely, he no longer needs "awareness exercises," since his awareness develops and expands by itself, from the very fact of the direct contact with nature. (Not for nothing do human beings live on the earth, with its unique form and conditions.) The lack of respect for nature, its destruction and damage, harm us directly. We need to feel nature directly and give free rein to all our senses. To feel nature to the point of linking up with it constitutes a natural state for the mind and soul, and even for the physical body. In this state, wonderful processes occur on the energetic level.

The reaction of the chakras to being in nature is extraordinary. Nature's action is very powerful because all the sounds and colors that we use for balancing the chakras are found in nature in exactly the way human beings need them for their body, mind and soul.

In the course of the book, many different exercises for balancing the chakras are presented. From experience and experiment, let us mention that the exercises for balancing the chakras that take place outdoors in nature are among the ones that most promote the balance, openness, cleansing and stimulation of the chakras, and daily practice of balancing the chakras in nature leads to far-reaching results. In addition to balancing the chakras, it helps us as human beings to establish deeper and more direct contact with our own soul, of whose existence many people are not even aware. By listening to the soul, we must also heed its call to protect, preserve and respect nature, and to recognize it as an entity that is inseparable from our own, both as individuals and collectively as the human race.

In order to balance our base chakra, we need the feeling of and contact with the earth. Without this, our chakra is liable to become completely unbalanced. In states of imbalance of the base chakra, and especially in states of lack, we recommend direct contact with the earth, which involves most of the senses.

The frequencies of the earth, the water sources, the plants and the animals have an opening and balancing effect on our first three chakras. They support the action of the chakras, reinforcing and stimulating them. This effect on the lower chakras supports the opening of the higher chakras and permits their balanced action. As we said before, besides the direct effect of the first three chakras, these frequencies lead to the development of our awareness of the soul and help us be more heedful of it.

The light and color of the sky, which wears frequently changing shades, both in the light of the sun, and in the light of the moon and stars, lead to the opening of the three lower chakras and to the increase in the action and openness of the upper chakras.

The exercises for experiencing nature that appear in the book should be performed in a state of calmness, openness, and tranquillity. (We call them "exercises" in this book, but they are actually states that are natural to our body, mind, and soul.) They are extremely simple, and the main point of them is being in nature with openness and observation. It is important to be in a state of acceptance in order to receive the sum total of the frequencies that open and cure and link up to us freely while we are in nature.

❋ CHAKRAS ❋

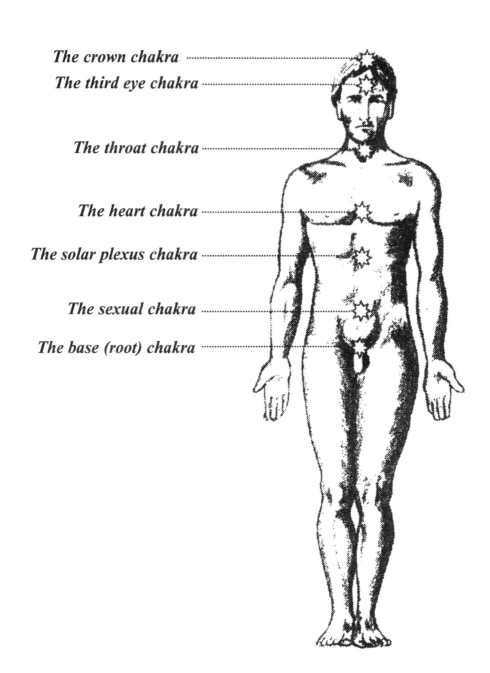

The crown chakra

The third eye chakra

The throat chakra

The heart chakra

The solar plexus chakra

The sexual chakra

The base (root) chakra

The first chakra

The base (root) chakra

Muladhara

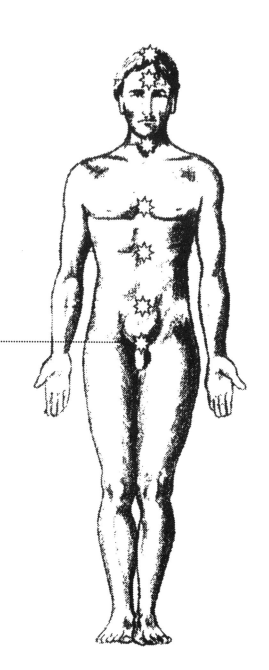

The base (root) chakra ⋯⋯⋯⋯⋯⋯⋯⋯⋯⋯⋯

Location of the chakra: In the region of the perineum – the point located between the genitals and the anus.

Colors: Red and black.

Complementary color: Blue.

Symbol: A circle surrounded by four lotus petals, with a square inside it. Sometimes, the square is colored yellow-gold, which symbolizes the material world, and it can contain the letters of the sound or mantra "lam." A stem emerges from the square, symbolizing the chakra's link to the central thread, the Sushumana.

Key words: Deep-rootedness, stability, acceptance, self-preservation, survival, perception.

Basic principles: Physical willpower for existence and survival.

Inner aspect: Being grounded.

Energy: Vitality.

Age of development: From birth to between three and five years.

Element: Earth.

Sense: Smell.

Sound: "Lam."

Body: The physical body.

Nerve plexus: Coccyx.

Hormonal glands linked to the chakra: Sexual and adrenal glands.

Body organs linked to the chakra: The "hard" organs of the body – the spine, the skeleton, the bones, teeth, and nails. The excretory organs – the anus, the rectum, the intestines. The birth and reproductive organs – the prostate glands and the gonads. Also, the blood and the cell structure.

Problems and diseases that occur during an imbalance of the chakra: Constipation, hemorrhoids, fatigue, apathy, lack of energy, blood problems, problems of stress in the spine, joint and bone problems, problems in the tissues, and skin problems.

Essential oils: Patchouli, cedarwood, sandalwood, vetiver.

Crystals and stones: Agate, ruby, onyx, hematite, red jasper, bloodstone, red coral, cuprite, garnet, jet, rhodochrosite, spinel, smoky quartz, alexandrite, black tourmaline.

Stars and astrological signs linked to the chakra: The base chakra is symbolized by the planets Mars, Pluto, and Saturn, and the signs of Aries, Taurus, Scorpio, and Capricorn.

Aries, the first sign of the Zodiac, symbolizes a new beginning, primeval life energy, power, and aggressiveness.

Taurus symbolizes the affinity for nature and earth, stability, passion, and the pleasures of the senses.

Scorpio symbolizes sexual power, transmutation, and renewal.

Capricorn symbolizes stability, gradual activity, and structuralism.

The base chakra, which is also called the root chakra, is located in the region of the perineum. Its petals point downward, toward and between the legs, and its stem points upward, toward the central thread – the Sushumana. In a healthy and natural state, it should be slightly open.

This chakra is our link to the material world. It conveys cosmic energies to our physical and earthly layers, and causes the stabilizing earth energy to flow into the energetic bodies. The base chakra is exactly what its name suggests. It constitutes the basis for the activity of the rest of the chakras, and for our existence, constitution, and development. It grounds us to the earth by safeguarding the nourishing and life-giving link with this source of power. It grants us a feeling of confidence and stability, which we need for our development on all levels. We are energetic creatures, and our souls are immortal, but when we come into this world, by dint of the karmic law that decrees that we have to go through various incarnations in order to repair our karma, we become part of the earth element that gives life to our physical body and nourishes it. The more securely we feel our roots embedded in the earth, the easier and simpler our physical lives in the material world become.

The base chakra stimulates our basic survival instinct – the need to work toward stability, which provides us with food, shelter, a family, and continuity, all of which are part of our role and needs in this world. Moreover, it is this chakra that activates the sexual instincts (as opposed to the awareness of sexuality, which is one of the functions of the second chakra). The sexual instinct is embedded in this chakra because of the need for continuity and self-preservation by creating an additional "shoot" from the basic trunk.

The base chakra represents the struggle for survival and self-preservation, and it is the source of all the instincts that exist in order to protect ourselves and safeguard our physical and mental health, as well as fulfill our basic needs. First and foremost – the "instinctive" desire and aspiration to protect ourselves against danger. Fears that prevent us from getting into a situation that can jeopardize our physiological or mental health are part of the self-protective mechanism that is activated by this chakra. Most of these fears are basic, and shared by all human beings, such as the fear of falling, of fire, of drowning, and so on. Various conditions of life – mainly competitive ones – cause the person to test the limits of these primal fears. In general, people do not put these basic fears to the test unless there is a desperate need to do so, or they are motivated by a competitive impulse and a need to prove their abilities. These are manifestations of a situation of imbalance in this chakra, often involving an unbalanced solar plexus chakra. Cases of imbalance in the survival instincts of the base chakra can lead to cowardice and dependence on the judgment and opinions of others – and, on the other hand, to going to extremes and taking exaggerated risks.

The age of the chakra's development

The age of the base chakra's development is from birth to age three or five. The fact that children tend to develop very quickly today as opposed to the previous generation – and certainly as opposed to earlier generations – must be taken into account. For this reason, the age of the development of the chakra may alter slightly. Of course, the chakra does not stop developing after those years, but those years are critical, and form the general shape of this chakra, similarly to the development of the rest of the four lower chakras. If the needs of this chakra are met properly during this period, it will function more easily and powerfully, and will be more open during all the stages of life. If its needs are neglected, there will be a need to focus on treating and balancing the chakra, since it will inhibit and disrupt the person's normal functioning in all layers, and, of course, the main functions for which it is responsible.

Those years constitute the basis of the person's development during all the periods of his life. The essential needs – nutrition, a roof over his head, warmth, stability and love – are essential for the proper development of the chakra, as well as for the general healthy development of the person. If these needs are not met during the person's first years of life, it will critically affect the overall functioning of the chakra. During those years, the child learns to know the physical world; he touches, feels, tastes. Therefore, he requires a range of stimuli, and a certain freedom of action – albeit not limitless – in order to be able to form his initial perception of the world, which is reflected later on in the functions of the chakra. The basis of his life is constructed during those years. He learns to know the world as nourishing, loving, warm, embracing, and safe – perceptions that affect the entire course of his life. The opposite may be true, however, when the child is not given initial security, the security of having his mother and father near him, ready and willing to feed him, care for him, help him, give him a hug, and protect and defend him, he is liable to experience the world as cold and alien, frightening and dangerous. Afterwards, unless very powerful corrective experiences occur, he is liable to develop a survival-oriented perception of the world, according to which he has to have instant gratification of his needs, and when this does not happen, he feels fear and emptiness. The lack of proper mental and physical nourishment in those first years, the lack of love, warmth and contact, are liable to create a kind of "bottomless pit," "a black hole" in the person that he is not able to fill with various material means, because he does not recognize the source of the lack that has created his many unfulfilled material passions.

Harmonious functioning of the base chakra

When the base chakra is open and operates harmoniously, the person feels a deep and direct connection to the earth and to the life forms in nature. He feels grounded in a positive way, connected to life, and full of interest. He feels stability, self-satisfaction, and inner strength. He is assertive, and can cope with conflicts and crises courageously. He can make decisions and act on them without any real difficulties; he is energetic, active, and discerning; he has healthy sexuality and a strong life force.

When the chakra is balanced, the person feels that the cyclical nature of the universe is perfectly natural, because this is the chakra that symbolizes new beginnings, ends, and cyclicality. The person feels the desire to shape his life himself, and build it, taking nature and the earth into account. Accomplishing material objectives is relatively easy, and he feels confidence in the universe and in the course of life. This feeling of confidence prevents worry about basic survival needs, because he feels that everything he requires can be found in the world and will be supplied to him. Moreover, when the base chakra is well balanced and open, the person can link the spiritual layers of the universe to the basic material actions of life on earth. This situation creates spirituality that is not "up in the clouds", but rather is expressed in all the person's moves and actions. He may feel that his head is in the clouds while his feet are firmly planted on the ground.

Unharmonious functioning of the base chakra

An imbalance in the base chakra is manifested in a disproportional focus on survival and material needs. All of the person's thoughts and interests are focussed on physical needs such as food, drink, sex, and money. These are likely to take first priority, and occasionally, in severe states of imbalance, to constitute the peak of his aspirations or his main source of interest. The person is liable to feel the need to satisfy his lusts without taking the consequences of his actions into account, because of a powerful and tangible urge to gratify these needs quickly. This state of imbalance of the chakra is likely to be expressed in sexual promiscuity and sexual imbalance. Moreover, the person may feel that he is unable to give or receive freely, either in material or emotional matters. He may focus partially or entirely on satisfying his needs, while ignoring the needs and feelings of other people. The greed for money is liable to take control of him, followed by the need to accumulate more and more material assets (which is never satisfied – somewhere deep down there is always a feeling of instability and a lack of confidence in the universe).

When the chakra is not balanced, various existential fears may emerge: fears of lack, of poverty, of physical deterioration, and so on, as well as severe anxieties. The person may be very "earthy" in the non-positive connotation of the word, to the point that matters that are not absolutely physical will be difficult for him to comprehend. People whose base chakra is not balanced are likely to be extremely egocentric, aggressive, and short-tempered. They may try to impose their will and opinions on others by force or aggressiveness, and feel rage, anger, or even violence when their desires are not fulfilled.

The colors of the chakra

The basic color of the base chakra is red. Red has the lowest frequency vibrations in the spectrum. The base chakra is responsible for producing the color red in the colors of the aura. When it is in a state of balance, the first chakra produces a vivid, glowing red color.

Red symbolizes vitality, action and warmth. Its properties symbolize the action of the base chakra – it stimulates, warms, invigorates, and increases vitality, evokes persistence, passion, and ambition. It dispels conditions of "being stuck" for the sake of movement and stimulates life energy. In color therapy, as we will see below, it is possible to treat the base chakra by projecting the color red, since red renews the chakra's stable functioning and encourages its stimulation and action.

Moreover, it helps treat many of the physical functions that are linked to the base chakra – it is used in the treatment of the circulatory system and stimulates the production of red blood cells, the blood system, the spinal fluid, and the functioning of the nervous system. It is used for treating various blood problems, and it is extremely effective in various treatment methods for balancing states of exhaustion that are caused by a lack or blockage in the chakra. It is used for treating arthritis, muscle pains and fractures, bacterial diseases and impotence, as well as for treating diseases of the sensory nerves, such as problems with hearing, taste, smell, sight, and feeling. It stimulates sluggish or static metabolism, and accelerates the excretion of toxins and metabolic waste. It helps alleviate constipation (one of the most common conditions of an unbalanced base chakra), expands the blood vessels, and helps in the production of blood.

As we said before, the base chakra is the one that produces the color red and causes it to flow into the field of the aura. When the chakra functions in a healthy, balanced, and optimal manner, the color red will appear in a balanced, clear and shining manner in the aura. In this situation, it attests to great vitality and good physical health, to inner strength and strong will power, to a warm and enthusiastic nature, independence and alertness, openness and extroversion, sentimentality, motivation, leadership ability, courage, passion, sexuality and sensuality.

When the base chakra is not balanced, the red color in the aura appears dull or in a state of excess, and in places where it does not natural belong, such as in the higher layers of the aura that are parallel to the upper chakras, and it is spread over the aura unevenly, or like a dark, muddy cloudiness. In such a case, it is liable to attest to aggressiveness, anger, violence, a destructive urge, vengefulness, frustration, confusion, rebelliousness, dominance and tyranny, insanity, hyperactivity, tension, and impotence.

When a light red color appears among the colors of the aura, it attests to sexuality, passion, eroticism, cheerfulness, femininity, sensitivity, and love. A dark red, crimson color attests to very strong will power, considerable physical strength, masculinity, courage, and leadership ability. When the chakra is not balanced, a "muddy" dark color may appear, attesting to rage, hostility, nervousness and aggressiveness.

Crimson, too, as well as brown, belong to the colors of the base chakra. Brown, when it appears in a clear, balanced manner in the aura, and in its right place (in the region of the base chakra, sometimes merging slightly with the area of the groin or the thighs), attests to roots, great stability and a strong link to nature and the earth. When it appears unevenly, and in any other location in the aura, especially those representing the upper areas of the body, it is not a good sign. In such cases, particularly when we see an obvious lack of balance of the base chakra, it is likely to attest to egoism, to difficulties in giving and receiving love, to excessive earthiness, to addiction to various things, and to disease and destruction.

The connection between the base chakra and the physical body

Every one of the chakras affects and is affected by the physical body, its functioning, and its health. This connection is mainly manifested in the action of the glands. Each of the chakras, with the exception of the base chakra, is linked to one of the subtle bodies.

The base chakra, with the lowest frequency, is connected to the physical, solid body, and to the most "solid" aspects of the body – the bones, skeleton, flesh, muscles. When situations of imbalance occur in these basic organs, the state of the base chakra must be examined.

Treatment of the chakra, and work with aromatic oils, crystals, colors, and various physical and psychological techniques, will lead to an improvement in the physiological condition by balancing the chakra and opening its blockages. Thus, these treatments can help with problems such as rheumatism, arthritis, and other joint and bone, tissue, and skin problems.

One of the symptoms that can indicate problems in the base chakra is the feeling of a lack of love – or even revulsion – toward one's body and its basic functions (such as a feeling of disgust toward our excretory organs, etc.). When the base chakra is properly balanced, the person knows his body, appreciates it, and accepts all of its functions naturally. A healthy base chakra inspires a feeling of appreciation toward the physical body, with its variety of marvelous and enjoyable activities. A feeling of physical power is built up inside us, the ability to move ourselves and use and activate our body as we like. However, a lack of appreciation for the body, or contempt for our physical layers, as well as for our physical needs such as eating, physical activity, excretion, motion, or sexual activity, requires an investigation of the state of the base chakra, and balancing it, if necessary.

When the base chakra is blocked or unbalanced, physical disorders in the organs linked to the chakra may occur – in the spine, skeleton, bones, legs, teeth, nails, sphincter, intestines, blood, prostate gland, and gonads.

Our back and spine represent the feeling of support that we experience, ostensibly externally – but we must remember that everything we experience "outside" of ourselves is a reflection of our feelings toward ourselves. States of imbalance in the base chakra are generally characterized by some kind of feeling of a lack of external support – a lack of support by those around us, which is always a mirror that reflects the support we give ourselves; or a feeling of a lack of support by the universe, which is expressed in a fear of the future, of a lack of money, of accidents, and so on. Since these feelings are so common, and many people feel that they have to "fight" for their lives in our current apparently competitive world, many people suffer constantly from back pains and slipped disks that stem from similar causes.

Two additional problems that are very characteristic of an unbalanced base chakra are constipation and hemorrhoids. Constipation symbolizes a basic problem in the ability to let go. Although it is very common, it should not be treated lightly. Constipation can lead to numerous complications, among them excessive toxins in the digestive system, flatulence, chronically deficient digestion, and so on. As we said previously, constipation symbolizes an inability to let go. This can be expressed in various behaviors: difficulty in letting go of money – stinginess; difficulty in releasing feelings – either in expressing them or in the inability to let go of past hurts; hoarding old things; maintaining relationships that are no longer supportive, and so on. On the mental, conceptual layer, this is likely to stem from the inability to let go of old, useless, and inhibiting thought patterns. When there is a problem of chronic constipation, it requires immediate treatment. It is not a "minor" problem, as people are inclined to think. In cases of chronic constipation that extend over long periods in the person's life, the root of the problem could lie in the age of development of the base chakra – some time between the ages of one and five, approximately. In any event, it is necessary to perform a deep balancing of the base chakra in order to solve the problem.

Sphincter problems also represent different layers of difficulty in letting go. The idea of difficulty in releasing often stems from the feeling of "I don't have, I won't have, if they take it away from me, I won't have anything," and so on. This is indicative of a basic lack of confidence in the universe, an inability to adjust oneself to the cyclical nature of nutrition and getting rid of waste products – excretion, letting go. Hemorrhoids also represent the fear of letting go – often of hurts that occurred in the past. They can also constitute the physical pattern of an emotional fear that there isn't enough time. Moreover, a lack of confidence in the universe – that it will provide us with everything we need, when we need it – lies at the root of the problem.

The base chakra is also linked to the bones and joints. The bones represent structure, basis. When the perception of the basis is shaky, it means that the person does not feel in harmony with the structure of the universe and its processes. The bones can suffer from different problems, and may sometimes indicate general states of imbalance and proper grounding. Scoliosis, which occurs in many people at the onset of adolescence and slightly prior to that, represents the same feeling of a lack of support by the universe, a lack of confidence in its processes, and an inability to flow with them harmoniously. Although it appears during adolescence, it generally develops during the preceding years, and only manifests itself later on. The way in which we grasp the universe's support of us – flowing with us rather than "against" us – is embedded in the first years of the chakra's development, and traumas at this age affect the general amount of confidence we have in life.

The joints, which move our limbs, represent flexibility and the ability to accept changes, which cannot be done harmoniously without a solid basis and a starting point from which we can keep on shaping our lives as we wish. Various joint problems, such as rheumatism and arthritis, require that the condition of the base chakra be checked and balanced immediately. Blood is also linked to the action of the base chakra. Blood is the essence of life, the essence of the physical body. A negative approach toward the various layers of life, hostility in its various forms, and a lack of happiness, deriving from an inability to understand the nature of our existence in the physical world, can lead to anemia and problems in coagulation of the blood.

The influence of the chakra on hormonal activity

The base chakra is linked to the gonads and to the adrenal glands. The gonads (the testicles in men and the ovaries in women) are part of the endocrine system. The hypophysis (in the brain) is the gland that oversees the action of the gonads "from above." At its hormonal command, hormones are released and various processes occur in the testicles and ovaries. The action of the gonads is necessary for performing some of the most basic functions of the base chakra: continuity, fertility, and maintaining the sexual instinct and its proper functioning.

When there are any problems in the functioning of the gonads and we diagnose sexual impotence caused by a hormonal or physiological source, as well as sterility, we have to examine the base chakra. In such cases, we treat, balance, and open the chakra, as well as use projections of the color red, and red stones. The color red stimulates the sexual layers into action, and helps in the treatment of impotence and sterility. A survey of the crystals and stones that are suitable for the base chakra reveals that many of them act in the same way. The aromatic oils that are suitable for work with the base chakra are likely to be very helpful in solving problems linked to the gonads and sexuality – fertility and instinctive sexuality, that is, sexual potency.

The adrenal glands clearly represent part of the most basic functions of the base chakra. They are located above the upper lobe of the kidneys and consist of an outer layer that produces steroid (fatty) hormones, and an inner layer that produces a protein hormone. Among the hormones that are secreted by the outer adrenal layer, it is important to mention aldosterone, which participates in the regulation of blood pressure by influencing the kidney, and works at keeping water and salts in the body, as well as cortisol, which is very important when there is an injury or an acute disease. Cortisol increases the amount of foodstuffs (glucose, amino acids, and fatty acids) in the blood, thus enabling the body to cope better with situations of stress. These two hormones are essential for life. Cortisol is an energetic generator, and is also responsible for storing energy, and regulates the element of fire in the body. Aldosterone, as we said, prevents the loss of fluids and maintains the balance between potassium and sodium in the body.

The inner adrenal layer secretes the hormone adrenaline into the bloodstream during states of mental or physical stress. The physical changes that adrenaline causes enable the body to cope better with situations of stress. Through this mechanism, the "fight or flight" response is activated. This response occurs in situations of stress, and was originally a primitive mechanism from the early stages of evolution, and was meant to prepare the body for battle or rapid flight in a life-threatening situation. We still have this mechanism. Today, when real life-threatening situations are relatively rare, it is activated in a variety of stress situations. In such situations, the adrenaline operates in parallel to the sympathetic nervous system and both mechanisms exert a similar effect on the organs. The adrenaline that is secreted causes an increase in heart and lung capacity, a broadening of the respiratory tract, a reduction of the blood flow to the skin, increased perspiration, an increase of the blood supply to the muscles, dilation of the pupils, and so on. All these reactions prepare the person for quick and immediate action. When the person is perpetually in situations of stress, this reaction will be activated repeatedly, thus causing an excessive use of the adrenaline supply, draining it faster than it can be replenished. Thus, the person may succumb to conditions of physical exhaustion and even collapse, and will require a great deal of rest and treatment in order to recover.

Situations of stress and tension are individual and relative. As real life-threatening situations are rare today, there should not be many reasons for activating this reaction. This is not the case, however. Many people tend to get stressed out for various reasons, and sometimes activate this reaction on a daily basis – while driving, at work, during a meeting with the boss, facing a deadline, in domestic arguments, coping with study and exam pressures, financial pressures, and many more reasons. Situations of stress that activate the "fight or flight" mechanism, constitute one of the main factors in weakening the immune system, as well as the functioning of the entire body. When the base chakra is balanced, and the person feels that life is supporting him, the chances of erosive activation of the adrenal glands are smaller. (The state of the solar plexus chakra is also very important, as it also affects the adrenal glands, and in a balanced state affords awareness and control of the various situations of stress.)

Meditation

Linking up to the base (root) chakra

Linking up to the base chakra enables us to feel the state it is in and check on its action at a particular time. Thus, we can tell when the chakra is not balanced, or when a blockage of some kind exists in it or is about to develop as a result of a certain trigger. In parallel, various triggers are liable to *lead* to blockages in the base chakra. Generally speaking, many people tend to relate negatively to these triggers, since they manifest themselves as anger, fear, and so on. However, the apparently fierce and unbalanced emotions that arise from a particular occurrence may actually serve as a very powerful tool for checking the state of our chakra. After we become familiar with the properties of the chakra, we can attribute certain feelings to being linked to the base chakra. Therefore, when they arise, we understand that the chakra is not yet perfectly balanced, and we have a good opportunity to bring up the issues that are linked to the state of imbalance and work with them in order to make peace with ourselves and with the world on the particular topic.

In order to perform the meditation, you will need 15-20 minutes during which you will not be disturbed by anyone. Perform the meditation in a quiet room. Drip a few drops of one or more of the oils that influence the base chakra into an essential oil burner, choosing the oil/s to whose fragrance you particularly respond.

Sit comfortably, "symmetrically," or lie down comfortably. Take several deep, slow abdominal breaths. Concentrate on each of your organs, from bottom to top, and see that they are relaxed. In order to ensure that the tension is released from them, you can contract your muscles tightly and then relax it, from your toes to your head.

After you feel calm and relaxed, concentrate on your base chakra.

Visualize it as a flower with four petals, with the stem rising through your coccyx and joining the central column, and the petals facing downward. See the chakra's red color and look at it. Pay attention to how the petals of the chakra look. Are they wide open or closed? Are some of them open and some of them closed? Look at the red color of the chakra. What shade is it? Is the color "clean" or are there dark spots in it? Is it vivid and shining, or pale and faded?

When the chakra is open and balanced, look at it in your mind's eye and see its petals wide open, its red color vivid, abundant, and glowing. If the chakra does not look like this, it is a sign that you need to work on balancing, opening or cleaning it – according to what you see.

After you have diagnosed the state of your chakra, you have completed the first stage of the meditation: identifying the state of your base chakra. It is possible that while concentrating on the chakra, certain thoughts and issues will arise. You can stop at this point and write down what you saw, felt, and thought. These issues may be linked to the reasons for the imbalance of the chakra.

The second stage is opening the petals of the chakra and cleaning and reinforcing its color using the power of the imagination. It is advisable to perform the second stage soon after the first, without taking too long a break. But you can also concentrate on the issues that you jotted down and work with them, and repeat the two stages together a day later. You may notice changes in the state of the chakra.

Look at the color of the chakra. See red light descending from above, penetrating your head and flowing down your spine. The red light descends to the base chakra, envelops it and moves around it. Pay attention to the direction of its movement. Is it moving in an anti-clockwise direction (in order to balance a state of overactivity in the chakra), or in a clockwise direction (in order to open the chakra)? If you notice spots on the chakra, let the red light envelop them, erase them, and clean them off the chakra. If the color of the chakra is weak and pale, let the glowing red light stimulate the color of the chakra and make it vivid and shiny. Now, concentrate on the chakra's petals one by one. When you notice a closed petal, see in your mind's eye how it opens when the red light envelops it. Open one petal after another, until all the petals are open.

Remain seated for a few minutes after completing the meditation, and get up when you feel the right moment has come.

You may not succeed in opening all of the chakra's petals during the same meditation. Conversely, you may succeed in doing so, but for various reasons, next time you perform the meditation, you will discover that while some of the petals have remained open, one or two have closed again. This is a natural situation, since the blockages in the chakra have occurred over several years, and sometimes tend to be deep. Now, however, you have a tool to diagnose the current state of the chakra, and you can continue to balance and open it, using other techniques, meditations, oils, crystals, and awareness work.

Every time you perform the first stage of the meditation, write down the thoughts, associations and feelings that arise in you, and they will help you discover some of the reasons for the imbalance in the chakra.

The second chakra

The sexual chakra

Swaddhisthana

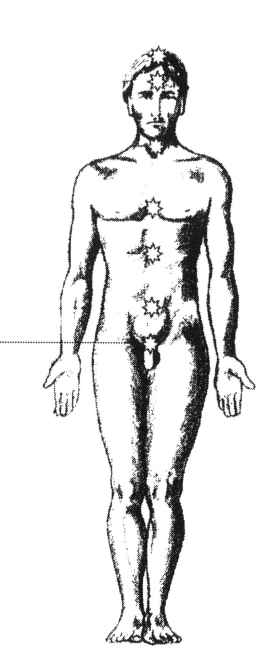

The sexual chakra

Location of the chakra: On the pelvis, between the pubic bones.

Color: Mainly orange, but also yellow leaning to orange.

Complementary color: Blue.

Symbol: A circle surrounded by five or six lotus petals. Sometimes another circle appears inside the first circle, containing the letters of the sound "vam." A stem emerges from the circle, symbolizing the chakra's link to the rest of the chakras and to the force of the universe. Sometimes a silver-gray half-crescent appears in the circle.

Key words: Change, sexuality, creativity, feeling of the other, honesty, inner strength, confidence.

Basic principles: Creative reproduction of the being.

Inner aspect: Emotions, sex.

Energy: Creation.

Age of development: Between the ages of three and eight.

Element: Water.

Sense: Touch and taste.

Sound: "Vam."

Body: Ethereal body.

Nerve plexus: Sacrum.

Hormonal glands linked to the chakra: The gonads – ovaries, testicles – the prostate gland and the lymphatic system.

Body organs linked to the chakra: The pelvis, the lymphatic system, the kidneys, the bladder, the muscles, the genitals, and all the body fluids: blood, lymph, digestive juices, semen.

Problems and diseases that occur during an imbalance of the chakra: Muscle spasms, allergies, physical frailty, constipation, sexual imbalance and lack of libido, sterility, inhibitions and repressions, lack of creativity.

Essential oils: Rosemary, rose, ylang-ylang, juniper, sandalwood, jasmine.

Crystals and stones: Amber, citrine, topaz, moonstone, fire agate, orange spinel, fire opal.

Stars and astrological signs linked to the chakra: The sexual chakra is symbolized by the moon, the planets Venus and Pluto, and the signs of Libra, Cancer, and Scorpio.

Libra symbolizes relationships that are based on partnership and equality, sensuality, creativity, and attention to the self.

Cancer symbolizes wealth of feelings, fertility, and acceptance.

Scorpio symbolizes sexual passion, sensuality, and transmutation by foregoing the ego in sexual unity.

The sexual chakra is also called the sacral chakra, and its Sanskrit name is Swaddhisthana. It is located on the pelvis, and its petals are approximately two finger-widths below the navel. Its stem reacts to the region of the sacrum and its nerve plexus.

The sexual chakra is the center for unfiltered primeval emotions, the sexual energies, and creativity. It symbolizes change and individuality through understanding the uniqueness of the other.

The energies of the sexual chakra are drawn from the base chakra and mingle with them. When the base chakra is properly balanced, stable, and established, it gives the sexual chakra confidence. When the principle of confidence is not balanced and anchored in the base chakra, this will affect the sexual chakra and its attributes. In such cases, the person may feel a lack of confidence toward himself and his abilities, but mainly toward the world around him.

Another of the most important functions of this chakra stems from the confidence the person feels toward the world: the feeling of the other. The meaning of this feeling is to include the other in our feelings, interests, and thoughts, in the same way as a mother feels toward her child, but according to the specific relationship. When the chakra is balanced, and it draws confidence from the base chakra, we can experience the other separately from ourselves, but simultaneously, as a part of us. We are sensitive and caring toward life around us, empathetic toward other people's feelings, considerate of them, of their desires, and of their emotions. All this happens when we feel like an independent and non-dependent whole, an individual. This attitude is acquired in the earliest days of childhood, and is affected by the way the parents relate to the child, and the way the environment relates to him. When the chakra is not balanced, a lack of caring about others can arise as a result of too much focus on oneself, or a state of dependency, or even a symbiotic relationship, when the person does not know where he ends and the other begins.

The sexual chakra is the center for sexuality, for sexual pleasure, including the awareness of fertility and sexual desire. As opposed to the base chakra, which is responsible for sexual instincts only, the sexual chakra is responsible for the broader sense of sexuality. The sexual chakra relates directly to the sexual act itself, and also to the manner in which we perceive our sexuality, to our acceptance of the gender into which we were born. It includes the way we accept and perceive ourselves as men or women while relating to social norms – taking into account the particular ages and periods of our lives. It is responsible for the awareness of sexuality, sexual choice, and the mass of emotions and associations that are connected with sex. Our sexual patterns are located in this energetic center, as are various patterns that have been imprinted on us by society. It is this chakra that absorbs the norms concerning sex and the attitude to sex that is prevalent in the young child's surroundings, whether they are norms of acceptance, naturalness and beauty, or feelings of sin and prohibition. The various beliefs regarding the man's "function" or the woman's "function" from the sexual and relationship points of view are "absorbed" into this chakra.

The sexual chakra is the seat of the ability to create, produce, give birth – producing something new and leaving a personal stamp. It is the seat of change, which is joined by curiosity, adventure, and innovation. Change and accepting change constitute a fundamental element in the development of the awareness – the ability to ask questions, not cling to what exists, to investigate and inquire about the unknown and the new. These are also the foundations of creativity. The sexual chakra is also responsible for our creative organs – the organs that give life to a new person, to a newborn baby, whose personality and being express his parents – physically, genetically, and mentally – on the one hand, and his individuality and state of being a separate entity on the other. This is creation – any creation. It is born in the person's innermost being, but the moment it is externalized, it has a life of its own.

The second chakra is the one that channels our inner abilities outward, and activates our inner strength, which is manifested in the ability to turn ideas into reality, to "activate" raw potential and turn it into something concrete – exactly like the child is raw potential when he is sperm and ovum, then a fetus in his mother's womb, and becomes a perfect, real being when he is born. The significance of inner strength is the ability to express our uniqueness, to realize our potential without being afraid of other people's reactions, without asking for permission and acquiescence, and using our talents fearlessly. This process is profoundly linked to the ability to recognize our power, and not to hand it over to others.

When we let others – who may be our parents, our surroundings, our mate, the "norms," the government, or any other factor – determine our personal attributes for us, and repress our inner feelings, beliefs, and abilities, we "hand over" to them the strength that is within us, because we forego its realization. This does not mean, of course, that these factors will take it from us by force. It is a question of giving inner permission to other people, out of a need for confirmation and acceptance, to judge us, to manipulate us, to persuade us to act in ways that are alien to us, possibly by smooth talking us. People tend to consent to this because of the need to "be like everyone else." But this is exactly the nature of the second chakra: the ability to "be like everyone else," to be a "part," without relinquishing our individuality and uniqueness, which are expressed directly in our unique way of thinking, our beliefs, and our feelings.

Often, people allow various factors, near or far, to force their negative influence on them and to affect their mature choice, because of this need to be part of society, and because of the fear of being ostracized. When the person is well aware of his inner strength, and his self-esteem and self-acceptance are strong, he does not permit manipulations of this type, and does not surrender his individuality for the sake of social acceptance. In contrast, he will respect the wisdom, experience, and talents of others, and will feel that they are giving him, teaching him, and reinforcing his personal strength through their ways of teaching. Having said that, he will not let the strength of human beings blind him, nor turn them into "gurus" at whose feet he surrenders the individuality of his being. States of imbalance in the sexual chakra can seriously affect the person's ability to stand up for himself and to adhere faithfully to the personal path that leads to self-fulfillment.

However, individuality does not mean turning one's back on society – on the contrary. When the sexual chakra is properly balanced, the person feels like an active partner in the shaping of his family, his community, and the society in which he lives, and aspires to function in it out of a desire to improve it and bring peace and tranquillity. The sexual chakra symbolizes the apparent duality of the wish to maintain our individuality but to be part of the whole. This duality, in fact, doesn't exist, because by being whole and perfect entities we are part of the universe in body, soul, and spirit. The changes that occur in the world affect these layers, directly or indirectly. Because we are energetically linked to our human brethren, to the earth, and to every form of life that exists there, we are responsible and influential, and we are also influenced by the changes in the universe.

When the person can live in peace both with his unique self, and everything that this involves, and with his surroundings and society, he can be honest. Honesty, both with himself and with his surroundings, is one of the functions for which the sexual chakra is responsible. Honesty is freedom from fear and anxiety. When the second chakra is well-balanced, the person can first and foremost be honest with himself. In many situations, human beings agree to delude themselves, to "turn a blind eye," to deceive themselves, for a variety of reasons. Many of these reasons stem from a lack of confidence in the universe. When the person is not sure that the universe looks out for him like a beloved child, or like an only child, many fears and anxieties about the future, about the other, creep in and take control of his soul. This leads to the person being unable to be honest with his surroundings. A lack of honesty stems from fear – the fear that telling, acting, and even thinking the truth will somehow lead to the person being hurt. When a person is confident of his inner strength, he is aware that nothing in the world can harm his soul if he expresses its truths.

The age of the chakra's development

The process of the sex chakra's development is greatly influenced by the young child's experiences between the ages of approximately four and eight. Since the child's development is individual, and depends on many factors, the initial age range may change slightly (starting from age three or five). The age range in which the chakra's significant development occurs is the period in which the child begins to discover his individuality.

During this period, the child tests his limits and those of his surroundings. While he requires appropriate limits to define his abilities, he also needs them to attain broad and correct freedom of action. The child needs a stable, warm and loving environment so as to continue building the basic confidence that affects the development of the base chakra. In order to revel in the joy of discovery and recognize the daily renewal of the world and its inherent adventures, the child requires a stable framework from which he can go out, and which defines and builds definitions that he can test. When the child's world consists of unexpected storms, an irregular lifestyle, and an unstable framework, he cannot see the beauty in the adventures that the world offers to all of humankind. Rather, he persists in his search, ever aspiring to some kind of stable and warm framework that was denied him during his childhood.

During those years, the child examines his primary link to his parents. On the one hand, he is dependent on them. He needs the physical and emotional security, the warmth and love, the direction and the instruction that they provide. On the other, he begins to discover and understand a little about his inner world, and begins to form personal desires that do not always coincide with those of his parents. He discovers that, despite the close tie between him and his parents, he is a separate creature. During this period, the importance of the respect with which his parents relate to his desires is great and significant. They do not have to accept and concur with all of his desires and demands, but they must respect the child's emotions and feelings, and allow him to feel that they accept his uniqueness and his emotions naturally, even if they do not always act in accordance with to them.

At these ages, the child begins to feel more and more a part of society. He goes to kindergarten and to school, feels the need and the desire to play with other children, to belong and to be accepted. In kindergarten and school, and when playing with other children, he learns the meaning of cooperation, sometimes by recognizing the conflict between his own desires and those of the others. He learns to cope and to find ways to act by balancing those desires, which are liable to be contradictory. Sometimes, of course, the attempt to cope fails, and this can cause emotional scars that greatly affect the balanced development of the chakra.

This is a period during which the child's curiosity about his sexuality is aroused. He begins to notice the differences between the sexes, ask questions, and wonder about them and about his sexuality. This is the period in which the child begins to be aware of being a "boy" or a "girl," and ask questions concerning society's demands regarding his/her gender. This is the period in which boys sometimes refuse to wear an item of clothing that is red or pink "because pink is a girl's color," and girls discover a difference between the type of games they favor and the type of games boys prefer. Having said that, it is important to mention that nowadays the labels imposed by society are beginning to fade, and more and more children are wearing "unisex" clothes, playing the same games, and taking an interest in various activities that in the past, for conservative social reasons, were gender-specific. During this period, the child also asks questions about "the facts of life" – how babies come into the world, how various things are formed, and so on – as a result of gradually increasing curiosity. "Why" questions become a routine part of the parent's life as the child demands answers, investigates, and displays curiosity. The child needs answers, and evasion or rejection is liable to undermine his confidence. However, even when answering him, the answer must be suitable for his level of understanding and sensitivity.

The environment in which the child lives, the way his parents behave toward him, and his upbringing during this period of development are very important for his inner strength as an adult. A strict environment, a strict upbringing, numerous unnecessary limits and unexplained prohibitions will harm the development of the child's personal strength. When we meet an adult who is unable to deal with the authorities or with various frameworks, has no self-control, is rebellious, or blames those frameworks for all of his problems, it is almost certain that problems originating in this period or in the unbalanced functioning of the sex chakra will be found.

Honesty, one of the other functions for which the sex chakra is responsible in the person's mind, is also formed to a large extent during this period. An environment that constantly judges the child, makes demands on him, and oppresses him with irrational prohibitions is liable to jeopardize his honesty. To the same extent, severe and illogical punishments may easily lead the child to seek shelter in lies. When the environment is excessively demanding, the child is liable to adopt its demands, which he finds difficult to meet. This makes him feel worthless and lacking in self-esteem. Similarly, when the environment does not respect his uniqueness, the child is liable to adopt the demands and norms that are forced on him as part of the characteristics of his personality. He aspires to these criteria and want to measure up to them, and this plunges him into a dizzying lack of honesty with himself. This situation becomes more acute, and when he becomes self-sufficient, he is liable to find himself still trying to satisfy the demands of his surroundings or of his family, and not actually expressing his most profound desires or operate according to them. Things like this are sometimes the reason for the person opting for an occupation that does not reflect his inner desire or his true talents, for a particular lifestyle, and even for a mate. In such a situation, the person lives with a continuing lack of honesty with himself, and feels dissatisfaction – which is sometimes incomprehensible – with his life.

Making many irrational demands on the child, as well as constantly judging him, naturally undermines his honesty. The child needs his parents and their love and acceptance. Knowing that he is liable to be punished or rejected for various deeds (sometimes the most natural deeds for a child of his age), he is liable to learn to lie and to persist in doing so. On the other hand, during this period, the children begin to be more and more aware of their parents' little "white lies." They are aware of the honesty that their parents demand from them, and are surprised to discover, more than once, that the parents themselves are sometimes capable of lying. The child does not distinguish between one lie and another. When he was punished for lying about who scribbled on the desk or who broke the window, he was surprised to discover that his mother greeted her mother-in-law warmly and flattered her, after hearing her say how much she loathed her. This is liable to evoke a crisis of a lack of trust in his parents as well as many questions. The child needs his parents to develop his ability to differentiate between good and bad and point his mistakes out to him. However, this must be done patiently, with respect and esteem for the child, out of a desire to teach and educate, and not out of an "adult's" will to punish or patronize him. Similarly, he needs a personal example, and the best way to teach him honesty is for the adults around him to be honest.

Traumas, oppression and unresolved conflicts at these ages harm the functioning of the sex chakra. This harm is liable to be reflected in the person's adult life for a long time, and affect all of his actions.

The sex chakra is strongly linked to the throat chakra, which is responsible for expression. When the sex chakra is not balanced, the person is liable to find himself in a situation in which he feels that he is not expressing his sense of self, his uniqueness and his personality. This situation leads to a feeling of dissatisfaction with life.

Notwithstanding, the sex chakra is essential; it expresses the nature of change and movement, and for that reason, curing and balancing it achieve good results that affect the person's entire being and effect a change in all areas of life.

Harmonious functioning of the sexual chakra

When the sexual chakra operates harmoniously, it expresses itself in vital and emotional movement in all areas of life. The person feels that he is an individual, recognizes his self, but is open to and accepts the feelings of others, and can connect to them easily. He connects to members of the opposite sex easily, and feels natural and comfortable with them. His attitude toward sex is healthy, natural, and logical. He does not use his sexuality or his exterior as a tool to accomplish his objectives, but as a way of expressing his profound emotions and connecting to and uniting with the one he loves. The person experiences passion that is healthy for life, an energetic flow of creativity, enthusiasm, and happiness. He can cope with changes and accept them with understanding, and even with joy, because he is aware that they constitute a springboard to a new life adventure. He is full of curiosity about life, and feels that the changes are a continuous and marvelous adventure. He is the one who is in charge of his life and influences others through a feeling of unity and caring. When the chakra is balanced, the person can express and feel natural and true emotions toward other people. He is independent, but at the same time aware of the feelings of those close to him, and sees himself as a part of the community and society, and as an active partner. He derives a great deal of pleasure from life, on all levels – sensual and sexual pleasure, pleasure from food and drink, and intellectual and spiritual pleasure.

Unharmonious functioning of the sexual chakra

Imbalance of the sexual chakra may derive from situations of imbalance in the age of development of the chakra, as well as from the period of sexual maturity. This period is fraught with feelings of insecurity concerning sexuality, with the search for oneself, and with attempts to define oneself as a member of a particular sex, and everything this involves. New sexual energies emerge in the person, and immediate society, parents and teachers are often incapable of providing the answers and teaching ways of channeling these energies. Often, these energies even cause damage via various unhealthy perceptions that cause the person to feel uncomfortable or ashamed of his feelings. This causes the adolescent to repress his feelings, to consider them unnatural and harmful, and damage his self-perception and esteem. Of course, the situation is more serious when the person grows up in a particularly conservative environment, where sexuality is accompanied by a feeling of "prohibition" or of sin deserving of punishment. His attempt to repress his sexuality, which he keeps to himself, causes tremendous conflicts, as does the desire to subdue the sexual energy that the sexual chakra activates, and the feeling of enjoyment and pleasure from life. These situations can cause gradual and continuous damage to his abilities to express himself sexually, to his sensuality, and to his ability to make healthy contact with the opposite sex. The state of an unbalanced sexual chakra may be expressed in a lack of joy of life, being "tired" of life, a lack of creativity, a lack of desire, inhibitions and complexes.

Of course, the repressed desires don't just "evaporate." They simmer beneath the surface. The conflict between desire – be it sexual desire, or the desire for self-realization or creative fulfillment – and its non-expression or the inability to express it, may cause a feeling of constant dissatisfaction and emptiness. The person may try to fill this void with various addictions – to money, food, alcohol, casual emotionless sex, and so on. When this chakra is unbalanced, the person feels restless and unsatisfied, and has difficulty finding his unique path in life and realizing it.

It may happen that the person yearns for a satisfying relationship, whether emotional or sexual, but is unable to find the correct channel for his emotions and passions. He may live in this way, lonely and without satisfaction, for many years, without being aware that the root of the problem is actually within him. This can stem from continual repression of emotions during childhood or sexual maturation, repression of sexual desires, or from voluntarily foregoing – sometimes unconsciously – the experience of these desires on the physical plane. The messages that are transmitted to the world declare that "I am unable to express my desires." A great deal of balancing work must be done both on the sexual chakra and on the emotional and mental layers in order to liberate these unconscious suggestions from the subconscious, and permit new relationships to develop. This occurs through an energetic transmission to the universe of the desire for and ability to achieve these satisfying relations.

To the same extent, repressing desires that should not be repressed physically and emotionally may be expressed in the unhealthy realization of these desires, in rushed, hurried sex that lacks any deep emotional relationship (simply in order to "get rid of" the physical sexual desire), in excessive sexual fantasies, in watching too many erotic movies, and so on. Sometimes these expressions are accompanied by guilt feelings or an addiction to sex – real or fantasy. In any case, tensions and a certain lack of confidence toward the opposite sex are obvious. This lack of confidence may manifest itself in extreme "over-confidence" and Don Juan-like behavior, but its root nonetheless lies in a basic lack of confidence toward the opposite sex and toward sexuality in general.

The colors of the chakra

The basic color of the sex chakra is orange. The sex chakra is responsible for producing the orange color among the colors of the aura. When it is balanced, the second chakra produces a vivid, bright and clear shade of orange. Orange provides us with stimulating and renewing energy while liberating us from obsolete emotional patterns. It is an invigorating color since it is a combination of red and yellow, and, like red, it is also warming and stimulating.

The color orange symbolizes warmth, self-confidence, happiness, cheerfulness, the ability to express oneself, energy, and motivation. It inspires joy, and increases self-confidence, the ability to make the most of mental talents, and striving to accomplish personal goals. Although it is a stimulating color, it affects the body in a soothing and antispasmodic manner.

The color orange affects the actions of the sex chakra and balances them in the person's body and mind. It disseminates joy, helps dispel sadness, melancholy and depression (which can be discerned when the sex chakra is in a state of lack), and disseminates courage, excitement and enthusiasm. It stimulates the ability to enjoy life, interest in life, adventurousness and curiosity. In addition to causing physical energy to flow, like the color red, it also balances intellectual qualities because of its frequencies that approach yellow. Orange particularly strengthens the ethereal body – the body that is linked to the sex chakra – and helps promote health in general.

From the physical point of view, the color orange helps treat many of the physical functions linked to the second chakra. It supports blood circulation and gently stimulates the body's fluids, contributes to the balanced functioning of the spleen and pancreas, helps treat various stomach problems, balances and stimulates the action of the digestive and renal systems, eases muscle cramps and strengthens metabolism. In addition, the color orange helps treat problems that reside in the range between the shades of red – the color of the base chakra – and the color yellow – the color of the solar plexus chakra. For this reason, it is effective when projected while treating problems of the respiratory and pulmonary systems, especially conditions such as asthma and bronchitis, and helps treat joint pains and problems. Since it is the color of calcium, orange is used for treating problems that are linked to calcium production in the body, such as osteoporosis and calcium-absorption problems. Since it is the color of the sex chakra, orange helps balance and treat a broad range of female problems: menstrual problems, fertility problems, sterility, sexual frigidity, and so on.

The sex chakra is operated by the color orange and transmits it to the electromagnetic field. When the chakra is balanced, orange flows and appears in the aura in a bright, clear and clean manner (that is, without cloudiness, blurring or brown or black spots in the region of the chakra). When the orange color flows in the aura in a balanced manner, it attests to creativity, self-confidence, practicality, practical intellect that can be applied in a concrete way, a plethora of ideas, innovation and inventiveness, a good ability to express oneself, gregariousness, balanced intellectual talents and good motivation. Conversely, when orange appears faded or cloudy in the aura field, or in inappropriate regions of the electromagnetic field, it may attest to exaggerated ambitiousness, competitiveness, a lack of sexual balance, excessive sexual lust that is not properly channeled, ignorance and aggressiveness, and the creation of unbalanced ties, sometimes based on some kind of rivalry. When the orange color that appears in the person's electromagnetic field or in the region of the chakra itself tends toward red, it may attest to a great capacity for enjoying life, intense enjoyment of a certain moment, great passion, sexuality, a lust for life, a need for a lot of physical action, and pride. When it is not balanced, it is liable to attest to arrogance and boastfulness. When the orange color in the electromagnetic field tends toward yellow, it may attest to a high degree of self-confidence, diligence and industriousness, keen and sharp intellect, wit, and the ability to use knowledge and intellect for practical purposes.

It is a good idea to project the color orange onto the sex chakra after an illness, during recuperation, when the person still feels slightly weak and lacks energy. When we feel a lack of energy, exhaustion or fatigue, and need a fast and effective "energy shot," it is helpful to project orange onto the chakra in order to stimulate vitality. To the same end, it is also possible to hang a piece of orange glass opposite the sun so that it projects the orange light onto the person.

The connection between the sexual chakra and the physical body

The sexual chakra is linked to the pelvis, kidneys, bladder, muscles, genitals, lymph, and all body fluids. For this reason, an imbalance in this chakra is liable to manifest itself in the deficient functioning of one of these organs and systems. This can be expressed in an imbalance in the body's circulation, in muscle problems, in kidney and gallbladder problems, and a broad spectrum of problems connected to human sexuality.

The kidneys, one of the principal organs for which the sexual chakra is responsible, represents shame, self-criticism and external criticism, disappointment, and a feeling of failure. Our personal yardsticks for success or failure, for "correct" and "incorrect," are in the main illusions that we ourselves have created. Our ability to accept the other, without criticism, judgment, or expectations, stems from our ability to behave in the same way toward ourselves – with self-acceptance. What is not acceptable to us is totally acceptable to someone else, and may even be part of the norms of another culture. Moreover, it is possible that in another incarnation, we ourselves perceived as natural and possible the very situation that we are condemning now in our present incarnation. For this reason, most of the borders, the limits, and the laws that we choose to believe in, may be illusions or excuses for a lack of self-esteem, reasons for self-condemnation. The sexual chakra is the source of joy, adventurousness, and the ability to see life as one long adventure that is packed with surprises – and so the errors, the mistakes, the disappointments, the guilt actually don't exist, because everything we experience is another adventure, lesson, or experience. When the sexual chakra is balanced and open, it does not mean that there will not be "disappointments" or "pangs of conscience." However, we can see things in the correct perspective, from the standpoint of self-knowledge and self-esteem. In this way, we know that even certain life experiences that we define as mistakes, as "incorrect", "negative", and so on, do not damage our self, because our self is not measured by "correct" or "incorrect", but rather simply exists in our particular way.

When the sexual chakra is not balanced, there may be a tendency for the person to measure himself according to his deeds, all the while criticizing himself and feeling that he has caused himself harm if he made a mistake. This leads to self-criticism, disappointment, and sometimes to shame, which are liable to continue for a long time, or become entrenched beneath the surface forever. In the same way that we perceive our experiences, we also perceive the actions of those around us, and criticize them or accept them as their own experience without defining it as "good" or "bad." Kidney stones and gallstones, too, often indicate profound and continuous self-condemnation.

The sexual chakra is responsible for the genitals, together with the base chakra which oversees the more physical layer of the organs. A substantial part of sexual problems that are not structural originate in clear mental causes. Our genitals represent our femininity or masculinity. As we said previously, the sexual chakra is responsible for the way in which we perceive ourselves as men or women. What does it mean to be a man? What does it mean to be a woman? Those are the questions that are asked in the energetic center of the sexual chakra. Is there suffering involved? Or heavy responsibility? What are the contexts and the associations that we have regarding the sex into which we were born in this incarnation? How did members of the home into which we were born relate to sex? How do we think our surroundings relate to sex? Are we resigned to our sex? Do we feel that we are really "a perfect woman" or "a perfect man"? Do we accept and love our genitals in the same way as any other organ in our body? Do we accept our sexual feelings as natural? These questions have an essential effect on the state of our genitals.

The age of the chakra's development is in one of the stages when the young child discovers his sexuality. A lot of people experience traumas at this age when, completely naturally, they discover their genitals, examine them, and enjoy them, but are "rewarded" with a torrent of disapproval from their immediate surroundings. The beliefs that prevail in the home and in society pertaining to sex and sexuality affect the person consciously more during adolescence, when the sexual conflicts are likely to be clearer and more obvious. The belief that sex is bad, that the genitals are "dirty", "you're not allowed to touch them," and so on, can create a conscious or unconscious feeling of rejection toward them.

It is astounding to think that for thousands of years, the prevailing opinion in various cultures was that the genitals were "dirty and evil." This attitude led people to reject and despise a part of their bodies, a part of themselves! Many of the problems connected to sexuality, as well as the various sexual diseases, originate in this perception, which we may carry with us from our childhood and adolescence – and possibly from previous incarnations.

Today's perception of sex can be confusing. On the one hand, tremendous emphasis is placed on human sexuality, and we see so much sexual permissiveness in the media that whoever is not "sexual" enough is liable to consider himself imperfect and incapable of living up to the norm. On the other hand, the old, conservative norms still clearly exist in various social strata – so much so that the situation sometimes smacks of hypocrisy and duality. The need to be "good enough" in bed is one of the reasons for sexual problems such as impotence, premature ejaculation, and tension, fear, and pressure during intercourse. Resentment and anger toward previous partners, out of a misunderstanding of the ways of the world – how we do or don't accept ourselves is reflected in our mate – are also likely to cause sexual problems. This is one of the reasons for vaginal infections, itches, and inflammations. Social beliefs, guilt, rejection of sexuality, the belief that sex and the sexual organs are dirty or "unworthy," tension, the desire to fulfill our partner's expectations from the sexual point of view (expectations that we ourselves contrive) and so on, all cause a large number of problems concerning human sexuality, the genitals, and the menstrual cycle.

In such cases, balancing the sexual chakra can be astonishingly strong, leading to far-reaching results, both in improving the deficient situation itself, and in adjusting the feminine or masculine self-perception and the perception of sex in general. Often, in order to treat the situation in the best way possible, it is necessary to bring up the traumas concerning our sexuality, directly or indirectly, examine them once again as another experience in this life, and free them lovingly. Balancing the chakra in conjunction with crystals, aromatic oils (that often help a specific problem), color projections, and Bach flowers, as well as meditations, guided imagery and other techniques, are likely to release sexual problems – even long-standing ones or ones that are considered to be "serious."

The influence of the chakra on hormonal activity

The sexual chakra is the chakra that affects the operation of the lymphatic system. This system helps cleanse the body of waste products. It helps transport protein to the capillaries and regenerate the volume of the blood plasma. It extends throughout the entire body, and consists of primary and secondary pipelines that become narrower until they are very thin pipes. There are various lymphatic centers that are responsible for different areas in the body. Lymph is part of the body's immune system. Bacteria and unwanted entities are trapped in the lymphatic centers, and the latter may swell up in certain cases of infection. This is one of the most important conveyor systems of the body. For this reason, when we ensure that the sexual chakra is well-balanced, we bring about a strengthening of the body, and increase its ability to fight external infections. The flow of the lymphatic system represents, as does the sexual chakra, our movement through life – the way we conduct ourselves in life.

Meditations

Linking up to the sex chakra

The meditation for linking up to the sex chakra is performed in a similar manner to the meditation for linking up to the base (root) chakra. Place an essential oil burner containing oils that are suitable for the sex chakra in the room in which you are going to perform the meditation. Sit or lie comfortably and relax your body. When it is relaxed and you feel calm and comfortable, concentrate on your sex chakra. Visualize it as a flower with five petals, its stem joining the central column in a horizontal line from the chakra to the spine, and its petals facing forward toward the groin area. See the chakra's orange color and concentrate on it. Pay attention to the color of the chakra (to its intensity, its cleanliness, its brightness, and its strength) and to its petals. Note which petals are open and which are closed. After you have diagnosed the condition of your chakra, you can write down your impressions for further work, as well as the feelings that arose in you while looking at the chakra.

Move on to the second stage of the meditation – opening the petals of the chakra, cleansing and strengthening the color of the chakra, and getting the chakra's energy to flow. Imagine orange light descending from above and penetrating your head, flowing along the central column of the chakras and descending to the sex chakra, enveloping it and filling it. It is possible that intuitively, without conscious intention, the light will move around the chakra in a particular direction. If not, move it yourself – in a clockwise direction if your sex chakra is underactive or weak, and in an anti-clockwise direction if there is an energetic overload in the region of the chakra. Look and see if there are any blockages in the chakra – dark spots, places where it is difficult for the orange color to flow, and so on. Concentrate on those places and make the orange light flow into them. See how it envelops the entire chakra, reinforces its color, and begins to open the petals one at a time. Continue like this, until you see all five petals open, and the color of the chakra is bright orange without any spots. Make orange light flow to all the blocked and motionless places. Let yourself feel the burgeoning strength that results from the stimulation and opening of the sex chakra for a few minutes. You may feel some kind of sexual arousal or stimulation – that is a natural process that attests to the opening of the chakra.

Continue with this process until you see the chakra's petals all open, and its color becoming orange without any spots or pale areas.

When you have finished the process, continue sitting for a few minutes. Slowly begin to feel the contact of your body with the chair; feel your legs and your arms. Move your legs a bit and open your eyes.

As we said before, it is possible that not all the petals will open up the first time you perform the meditation. Do not despair, but rather trust your personal process, and perform the meditation several more times. The impressions that arise during the meditation are important for understanding the reasons or the background for the various blockages in the chakra, so it is worthwhile writing them down and doing appropriate emotional or physical work using the various techniques for supporting the sex chakra.

Movement meditation for opening the chakra

Movement meditation helps us link up to the chakra's energies, increase them, and use their powers. In order to perform the meditation, you need an object-free room in which you can move lightly for 20-30 minutes, during which you will not be disturbed. You will need lively music – dance music or joyful Oriental music. Place the tape deck beside you or stand next to it at the beginning of the meditation so that you will be able to turn it on at the right moment.

Begin the meditation standing up. Take a number of deep breaths and close your eyes. See a stripe of orange light descending from above and penetrating your head, continuing down your spine and reaching your sex chakra, filling it with orange light. With each breath, see the orange light moving and growing, and taking on the shape of a ball. During exhalation, move the ball slightly. Feel the incredible feeling of the energy in the region of the sex chakra. Open your eyes and feel your posture.

Standing, move your legs slightly apart and bend your knees a bit so that you can push your pelvis forward. Make a few forward and backward pushing movements with your pelvis, making the movements slowly, and concentrating on the feeling in the region of the pelvis and groin. Turn on the tape and close your eyes again. Look at the illuminated orange ball in the region of your sex chakra. With the music, begin to move your pelvis in circular movements, like a belly dancer. Let the music sweep you away and control your movements. Move the rest of your body parts – your abdomen, arms, and legs – along with the movement of your pelvis. Your swaying pelvis leads the movements. See how the ball of orange light moves with your swaying pelvis, which "plays" with it, moves it from side to side, and bounces it as if it were resting on the pelvis. If you feel like expanding the dance by adding more movements, do so, since your sex chakra is being aroused.

After about 20-30 minutes, sit down and rest. After that, write down the feelings you experienced during the meditation. Did you feel joy and pleasure? Or did you experience shame and fear when performing the "suggestive" pelvic movements? Were the pelvic movements free or hesitant and calculated? The fear of expressing the power of the sex chakra interferes with its action and keeps it in a state of less than optimal openness. If you found it difficult to liberate yourself the first time you performed the meditation, try it a few more times, until you feel the awakening of the full strength of the sex chakra. If you performed the meditation easily and freely, you will almost certainly feel full of strength, joy, vitality and motivation afterwards.

The third chakra

The solar plexus chakra

Manipura

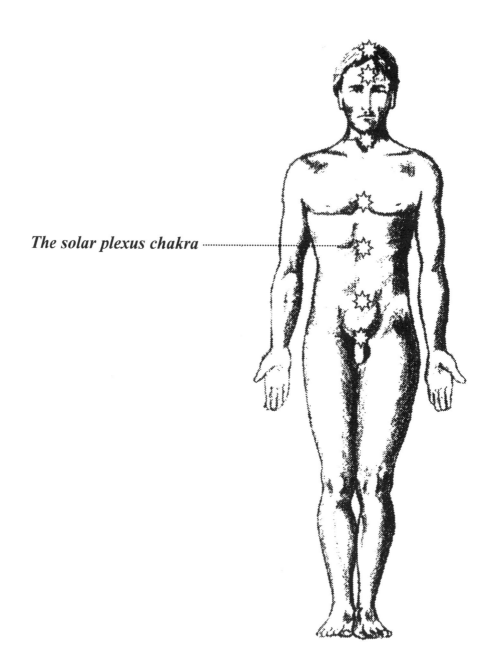

The solar plexus chakra ⋯⋯⋯⋯⋯⋯⋯⋯

Location of the chakra: Below the diaphragm, from the sternum to above the navel.

Color: Yellow.

Complementary color: Purple.

Symbol: A circle surrounded by ten lotus petals, and inside it a triangle (generally red in color) containing the letters of the sound "ram." A kind of stem emerges from the triangle, describing the chakra's link to the central thread, to the spine, and to the rest of the chakras.

Key words: Assimilation, self-knowledge, logic, cause, doing, integration, personal strength.

Basic principles: Forming the personality.

Inner aspect: Desire.

Energy: Inner strength.

Age of development: From two to twelve.

Element: Fire.

Sense: Sight.

Sound: "Ram."

Body: The astral body.

Nerve plexus: The solar plexus.

Hormonal glands linked to the chakra: The pancreas and the adrenal.

Body organs linked to the chakra: The respiratory system and diaphragm, the digestive system, the stomach, the pancreas, the liver, the spleen, the gall bladder, the small intestine, the suprarenal glands, the lower back, and the sympathetic nervous system.

Problems and diseases that occur during an imbalance of the chakra: Mental and nervous exhaustion, seclusion, problems establishing contacts, gallstones, diabetes, problems in the digestive system, ulcers, allergies, heart problems.

Essential oils: Juniper, vetiver, lavender, bergamot, and rosemary.

Crystals and stones: Citrine, amber, tiger's eye, peridot, yellow tourmaline, yellow topaz, watermelon tourmaline.

Stars and astrological signs linked to the chakra: The solar plexus chakra is symbolized by the sun, the planets Mercury, Jupiter, and Mars, (Mars symbolizes activity and energy, assertiveness and power), and the signs of Leo, Sagittarius, and Virgo.

Virgo symbolizes analytical prowess, the ability to classify, acceptance of conventions, devotion, and service.

Leo, whose planet, the sun, symbolizes the splendor of the solar plexus chakra and affects it, symbolizes the qualities of the chakra that express strength, status, the need for recognition, warmth, power, and abundance.

Sagittarius symbolizes abundance, growth, and expansion, wisdom and experience.

The meaning of the Sanskrit name of the third chakra, Manipura, is "the diamond palace." The location of the chakra is the solar plexus, which is in the region of the diaphragm, and extends below the sternum to the navel.

The solar plexus chakra symbolizes our sun – the center of our personal strength. We absorb the life-giving and stimulating strength of the sun into this chakra, and as a result create an active link with the rest of humanity and with the physical world. The chakra is responsible for the development of our personality and the transmission of our emotions to the world. It directs our ability to influence our surroundings, our inner strength, and our intellect in its practical aspect. Via the solar plexus chakra, we connect to the world and interpret it according to the state of the chakra, and our emotions. It is the center of personal strength, desire, ego, and self-realization. Relationships with other people, the ability to enter long-term, balanced relationships, our desires, the things we love, and conversely the things that we do not love – most of these are directed by this chakra. This chakra directs our desire for recognition and for social standing, as well as for a clear identity in society, desire and aspiration for power, achievement, and for realization of our goals and aspirations, as well as for adopting social patterns.

This is the chakra that represents the ego. Part of our personality or ego is linked to building a rational attitude and to expressing a clear opinion about life, deriving from the ability to shape and form personal opinions. In order to have the ability to decide about life, ranging from the simplest things to the loftiest topics, we need to have an independent ability to form a personal opinion. Through the decisions we make in life, we are able to fulfill our potential completely. The process of defining personal power begins with the second chakra. It continues to the solar plexus chakra by creating a tighter link with the intellect and rationalism, which we use for forming an opinion and for making decisions concerning our world. The search for our individuality and self-definition, which begins with the sexual chakra, continues through the constant struggle with the reality of society's expectations of us, the social norms and conventions among which we search for our "personal line," which is not always in agreement with these conventions. We need the rationality, logic, and resoluteness of the solar plexus chakra in order to develop this personal line for ourselves.

The solar plexus chakra enables us to assimilate knowledge and experience. All the experiences, events, acquired knowledge, and empirical knowledge shape our personality and make us into what we are. Via this chakra, we grasp other people's frequencies and act accordingly. (In parallel, when we feel negative energies, the action of the third eye chakra cautions us against possible danger.)

The solar plexus chakra also has an extremely important role in our expressed spirituality. One of the chakra's most important functions is purifying the wishes and desires that are channeled from the lower chakras, consciously, by using the creative energy of those chakras for spiritual development, and for the transition to the higher chakras. From the spiritual point of view, the function of this chakra is to help us realize our vocation in the material world – to perform our life's function to the best of our ability by using our talents and capabilities, and to walk along our personal path of destiny in the material world to achieve self-realization in all the layers.

Via this chakra, the desires and passions of the lower chakras – the first and the second – are expressed and translated into a higher energetic mold that shapes our personality by connecting to the energy of the higher chakras.

Accepting and integrating feelings, desires, wishes, and expectations helps the third chakra become balanced and develop, because it increases the inner light and illuminates the situations and events that occur in our life.

When there is stagnation or blockage in the solar plexus chakra, the intuitive abilities do not flow smoothly to the higher chakras, and become concentrated in the lower layers of existence, by preoccupation with and focus on the material world. While this is happening, these abilities become limited. They will only become real spiritual abilities when they join and combine with the energies of the heart chakra and the third eye chakra.

When the third chakra is open, our ability to receive light (and permit it to illuminate and glow within) is great and affects all of our functions. We feel happy, satisfied, and content. When the chakra is blocked or unbalanced, we may feel sad and even generally unbalanced. In addition, we transmit these states to our outer world, and make it gloomy and sad – or conversely, bright and filled with light and happiness.

Through inner wholeness and our ability to receive light, the third chakra gradually converts the yellow light of the solar plexus chakra, which expresses intellectual comprehension, into the golden light of wisdom, knowledge, and abundance

The age of the chakra's development

The age of the solar plexus chakra's development is from age eight to twelve or thirteen. At this age, highly significant changes are taking place in the child's mind. He wants to be more independent, and he is already more or less involved in a social life outside of his parents' home – school, friends, and so on. Although at this age the child wants more independence, he still needs the warmth of his home. Many people of that age who were sent to boarding-schools or taken out of the world of childhood and forced to "grow up" faster experience many difficulties, psychological problems and states of imbalance of the solar plexus chakra later on.

At this age, the child's ego is growing and developing, as is his self-perception. He becomes more demanding, in a different way than during his earlier childhood years. He begins to develop awareness of various social conventions, wants to be "popular" with his friends and at school, and wants to build a certain status for himself – by means of success in his studies, his appearance, his parents' status, his clothing, and so on. His developing intellect causes him to accumulate more and more facts about the world, and the knowledge that was previously taken for granted now evokes questions and a need to test and investigate. Information is digested and absorbed more consciously and in greater quantities. At these ages, the child feels a need to make some of his own choices. He demands a certain freedom regarding his decisions, forms a certain social circle of which he feels a part, and is sometimes expected to contribute to the family by doing various chores. The interaction with the world, which was mainly based on acceptance when he was younger, begins to be two-sided, and the child is expected to give, to understand, and to take into consideration the feelings of the people around him – consideration that was hitherto minimal because of his young age.

Various cultures celebrate the transition from childhood to youth, symbolizing the beginning of the child's adolescence, with the transition from this life cycle of the solar plexus chakra to the cycle of the heart chakra. Since at these ages the physical and even mental development of girls tends to be faster than that of boys, the bat-mitzvah (in Judaism) is celebrated for girls at age 12, and the bar-mitzvah is celebrated for boys at age 13. In African and Native American cultures, too, there is an initiation ceremony that symbolizes the transition from childhood to adulthood at age 12 or 13. The initiation ceremonies symbolize the beginning of the acceptance of the responsibility, chores, and obligations that begin to form the child's yardstick vis-à-vis his personality and the way he meets society's expectations.

Harmonious functioning of the solar plexus chakra

The harmonious functioning of the solar plexus chakra creates a feeling of tranquillity and inner harmony. When the solar plexus chakra is balanced, the person can contain his emotions and cope with his feelings, desires, and expectations of life. He considers his emotions to be an important and vital part of his development, and knows how to accept them in proportion. He does not react in an overly emotional way, but on the other hand does not curb his emotions. He is able to combine his emotions, wishes, experiences, and expectations of life into a whole. He feels at one with himself, with his role in life, and with his surroundings. He accepts himself while respecting the nature and emotions of others. The person's deeds are harmonious, exist in conjunction with the laws of the universe, and increase his abundance and satisfaction with life. But not only his. A person whose solar plexus chakra is properly balanced can feel an affinity for and unity with the rest of humanity. Their desires and feelings, just like the quality of life of those close to him, are important to him, and his actions and decisions include and take into consideration the good of those around him. The person feels energetic, active, assertive, independent, and tolerant.

When the solar plexus chakra is balanced, the person is enveloped in inner light that protects him from external negativity and from negative vibrations in his surroundings. The person feels sure of himself; he is courageous and creative, has a strong personality, and radiates inner strength and self-respect.

Unharmonious functioning of the solar plexus chakra

A state of imbalance in the solar plexus chakra is manifested in the person's fierce desire to control both his inner and his outer world. His ego is unbalanced, and his need for status and respect is extreme, to the point where he is liable to hurt others in order to attain respect and power. Manipulative behavior, abuse of power, arrogance, and extremely domineering behavior are likely to occur when the chakra is not balanced. The person feels the need to accumulate and hoard more and more power, and becomes excessively competitive and ambitious. Many of the people who are capable of trampling others underfoot on their way up the ladder of success suffer from an imbalance in this chakra.

When the chakra is in an unharmonious state, the person feels perpetual restlessness and dissatisfaction. This state may often be caused by a lack of acceptance during childhood and adolescence, leading to an inability to form honest and genuine self-esteem. The feeling of worthlessness induces a need for constant action in order to conceal it from the world, so that the person judges himself over and over again according to his success in the material world. He becomes horribly ambitious and needful of material achievements and success in order to feel worthy and to "prove" his worth to other people. This situation can make it difficult for the person to calm down; alternatively, it can get him into a state of inactivity and restlessness. The person is liable to feel that he requires constant action in order to feel worthy and adequate.

In these situations, status and material success may be the person's focal point to such an extent that he rejects the emotional world as being of very little importance to him. He may even tend to ignore or repress emotions that "get in the way" of this perpetual pursuit of success in the material world. He does not succeed in repressing them or attempting to make them go away, of course, and for this reason, all those repressed emotions are liable to burst out in various situations. The person is unable to control these outbursts, which may hurt him and, in many cases, other people. In many situations of an unbalanced solar plexus chakra, feelings of rage and bitterness toward parents and the world fester under the guise of a poker face, with the person pretending that "everything's fine" in order to appear successful and happy in the eyes of the world. However, the repressed feelings give him no peace, and he may suffer from bouts of depression or rage.

When the person perceives his inner strength and power as a means of control, a natural chasm separates him from the rest of humanity. He creates the "I – them" dichotomy. He classifies "them" into categories of "those who can help me accomplish my objectives" and "those who get in the way of accomplishing my objectives." He often establishes ties based on various interests, but is incapable of creating close and genuine social relationships. He feels as if he is one against many, against the world, and not a part of or partner in it.

His efforts to control and manipulate lead to a loss of a great deal of energy, and the person may find himself exhausted, needing external stimulants such as coffee, sweets, and so on, to the point that he needs them constantly.

Cases can arise in which the person is afraid of his inner strength. This fear leads to constant self-criticism, which is tiring and exhausting, and causes him to be cold and restrained (this derives from a basic lack of confidence and from self-criticism). In fact, the person is going against the chakra's natural energy, which is warm and full of enthusiasm.

The colors of the chakra

The color of the third chakra is yellow. Yellow symbolizes the sun's light, which activates and "warms" the solar plexus chakra. When the chakra is balanced, it emanates bright, clear and clean yellow light into the aura field and absorbs the sun's energy and light. Yellow is mainly a "mental" color. It stimulates the intellect and the memory, and reinforces the ability to learn and organize. It symbolizes the ego and self-discipline, but also increases cheerfulness and lightness. Yellow is known as a reviving and comforting color that dispels sadness and depression. When yellow activates the solar plexus chakra in a balanced way, and the chakra is open to receiving it and balanced for emitting it into the aura field, it is possible to see it clear and bright in the aura field, without any kind of cloudiness or blurring. In this state, it attests to a strong personality, harmony, honesty, organizational ability, balanced self-discipline, balanced careerism and good business acumen, superior intellect, knowledge, a developed learning ability, an ability to examine things scientifically and analytically, and a diplomatic and tactful approach. When we discern an unbalanced or faded yellow color in the aura field or in the region of the chakra, or the color is clouded with dark or brown spots or sullied in any other way, it attests to problems in the solar plexus chakra that are liable to be reflected in an unbalanced ego, selfishness, a critical nature, obstinacy, excessive emotional control, intolerance, skepticism, cynicism, ignorance, laziness and a tendency toward depression.

Yellow has a powerful and stimulating action on the nervous system and the brain. It stimulates the motor nerves and muscle energy. It is possible to treat a range of problems linked to an imbalance of the solar plexus chakra by projecting the color yellow. This is because the chakra is linked to the liver, the gallbladder, the stomach, the large and small intestines, the lungs, the prostate gland, the thyroid gland, and the bronchial tubes. It exerts a stimulating effect on the kidneys and liver and helps treat the digestive system, problems in the nervous system, and imbalance of the thyroid gland. Moreover, it helps produce hormones, enhances the action of the intestines, the spleen, the stomach and the bladder, and stimulates the cleansing of the body via the liver. Its action on the digestive system, which is significantly affected by the solar plexus chakra, is excellent, and it reinforces the entire digestive system. It stimulates the digestive juices and the flow of the lymph fluids, purifies the blood and helps preserve and treat the skin.

Yellow can be used for treating psychological and mental problems such as depression, melancholy, mental exhaustion and a lack of concentration, as well as memory problems.

When we see a clear yellow color in the aura field or in the region of the solar plexus chakra, this can attest to the person being calm and open, with a strong and balanced personality, clear thinking and innovative attitudes. When the color of the chakra tends toward ocher (a slightly brownish yellow), or when the ocher appears in the colors of the aura, it means that the person is stable, practical, feasible, a bit earthy, thrifty and very self-disciplined. When the ocher appears unbalanced, this can attest to many inner pressures, extreme self-discipline, selfishness and cheapness, and sometimes a fierce need for control.

The connection between the solar plexus chakra and the physical body

The solar plexus chakra affects and is responsible for the action of the diaphragm, the respiratory system, the stomach, the pancreas, the gallbladder, the small intestine, part of the large intestine, the adrenals, and the sympathetic nervous system.

The chakra's yellow color affects our sympathetic nervous system, and the emotions that are trapped in it affect the functioning of the respiratory and digestive systems. The solar plexus chakra is closely linked to the digestive process and the digestive system, and it is the main chakra that influences its action. The way we "digest" life, via the characteristics of our solar plexus chakra, has a significant influence on the digestive system. In the same way that we examine our world via this chakra, classify, absorb or emit the things that we encounter in our lives, so the digestive system is responsible for "classifying" foodstuffs. The liver is responsible for examining the food after it has been digested, for separating the valuable substances from the worthless ones, while the stomach digests the foodstuffs, and the intestine helps expel the waste products. This system operates in a manner that is parallel and similar to the absorption-storing-release of emotions. When there is an imbalance in the "digestion" of emotions, it is generally possible to identify situations of imbalance in the digestive system.

Allegorically, the liver symbolizes anger and the way we cope with it.

When the gallbladder functions deficiently, it may attest to stored grudges or jealousy. On the emotional level, gallstones can stem from feelings of pride, critical behavior toward others, and constant condemnation, external or internal, as well as from feelings of bitterness and "non-accepting" thoughts about others.

The pancreas symbolizes the sweetness of life. When the person feels that life is "bitter" for him, when he feels a desperate need for sweetness and affection, it is possible that pancreatic deficiency or even diabetes will occur.

The intestines represent our ability to release emotional waste, and to get rid of emotions that are no longer useful to us.

Many of the emotions of anger, helplessness, sadness, and loneliness, as well as various fears, originate in childhood. The mature person no longer needs these emotions. He is now a self-standing person who is no longer dependent on his parents or surroundings. Having said that, many people tend to hold on to these feelings, and do not release them. They allow this store of emotions to damage the way in which they perceive the world and their energetic transmission that shapes the reality of their lives. Intestinal problems frequently attest to the inability to release the old, the unnecessary emotional waste, and sometimes even the superfluous physical waste. This state may be combined with another state of imbalance that characterizes the disharmony of the solar plexus, which is stinginess and the inability to let go of material assets. In addition, when there is any kind of imbalance in the base chakra, the person also has existential fears and a need to hoard, and sometimes finds it difficult to get rid of things that he absolutely does not need.

The respiratory system represents our ability to inhale life – to operate in it, to flow with it, and to move in it. When the chakra is in a state of lack, the person is liable to allow life to flow past him without being involved in it by expressing his personal action and desires. In contrast, when the chakra is in a state of over-activity, the person is liable to "devour" life instead of inhaling it in a healthy and balanced manner. Both of these situations can manifest themselves in fast, shallow breathing, as well as in problems of the respiratory system.

When the solar plexus chakra is in a state of imbalance, this can be expressed in problems in the abovementioned organs, as well as in allergies and eye problems. Allergies, on the emotional level, can stem from an attitude of dislike or fear toward the world. They can also stem from the denial of personal power or inner strength, or oppression, as can happen in situations of imbalance of the chakra, and especially in cases of deficient functioning of the chakra, where it expends most of its energies on activities that are not in the least positive for the person. The eyes represent our world-view, the way we look at the world. Eye problems may indicate, in one way or another, our fear of looking at what is happening in front of us, or our hostility toward what we are looking at. Moreover, it may indicate a disproportionate view of various events in our lives.

The influence of the chakra on hormonal activity

The solar plexus chakra is linked to the activity of the adrenal (suprarenal) glands and to the pancreas. (See the chapter on the base chakra for a detailed description of the adrenal glands.) In the context of the solar plexus chakra, it is important to mention the activity of the suprarenal glands in the stress process. When we focus on the solar plexus chakra and begin to balance it, we learn to notice that our stress reactions are individual, and depend on the proportions that we attribute to various situations in our lives. Thus, they can be controlled and altered. When the solar plexus chakra is balanced, the person can avoid getting into repeated situations of stress. He is generally calm, self-confident, sure of his inner strength, and less susceptible to external and internal pressures. By balancing the chakra, it is possible to reduce and prevent stress as well as physical breakdowns and exhaustion that result from frequent stress.

The pancreas is an exocrine gland (a gland that secretes its product into the digestive tract or onto the surface of the skin and the mucus membranes) that secretes digestive juices into the duodenum. It is also an endocrine gland that secretes hormones into the bloodstream. The endocrine cells are located in structures that are called Islets of Langerhans. Those are clumps of cells inside the exocrine tissue of the pancreas. The pancreas secretes two main protein hormones whose action in regulating the glucose in the body and the feelings of repletion and hunger is absolutely vital. The first hormone is insulin, which is secreted as a result of a rise in the glucose level after a meal, causing the glucose to enter the cells. This in turn causes a decrease in the glucose level in the blood. In addition, it serves as a signal for the body's repletion, and causes the surplus foodstuffs to be stored, thus encouraging the free use of glucose for various purposes. In a state of hunger, a decrease in the body's glucose level causes a reduction in the secretion of insulin from the pancreas, and an increase in the secretion of other hormones that constitute a signal for hunger.

The second hormone, glycogen, is one of the important hormones that serve as a signal for hunger. The decrease in the insulin level, and the increase in the glycogen level cause the glucose level in the blood to remain constant, despite the continuous consumption of glucose by some of the body's tissues. A constant glucose level is essential for the body, since there are tissues (especially the brain) that must receive a steady supply of glucose. Because of the close link between the action of the solar plexus chakra and the pancreas, the balancing of this chakra is essential in cases of diabetes and problems in the insulin and glucose supply.

Meditations

Linking up to the solar plexus chakra

(for cleansing it, releasing unwanted energetic burdens, and regaining personal strength)

In order to recognize our solar plexus chakra and identify the way it works, its power, and its current state of balance, As we did in the previous chakra exercises, here too we should have a notebook at hand in which we can write down our feelings and the visions and insights that occur during the meditation. It is also advisable to read through the meditation carefully before performing it.

Since the solar plexus chakra is the seat of the emotions, it often requires a "spring-cleaning," since various repressed emotions and inhibiting and negative feelings are liable to be trapped in it. These feelings may emerge during the meditation. We must not panic or feel uncomfortable: This is one of the objectives of the meditation, and it helps us know ourselves in depth. When these feelings emerge, it is a good idea to say aloud, or in your heart, "Thank you, I love you." This sentence represents our self-acceptance. When we accept ourselves in our entirety, we also accept those facets of our character that are seemingly undesirable to us or inhibit us. When we accept these facets completely, they become light by dint of the acceptance itself. Fear, anger, control, irritability, and so on do not exist separately from and independently of the light. They are simply the extreme edges of the light, which we perceive as darkness. The source of all emotions is love. However, when expectations are added to love, love becomes anger (in other words, anger is love with expectations). Unfulfilled expectations, a situation of "I didn't get what I wanted," are expressed as anger. Hatred is love with control. When we make love conditional, when we try to control love in accordance with conditions we laid down – you must do such-and-such so that I'll love you (we are liable to say this sentence to ourselves, too, consciously or unconsciously), we receive hatred, rejection or limitations (since we do not believe that love, even love for ourselves, can exist without fulfilling these conditions). If we explore the emotions in depth, we will discover that they are just love with an "extra." When we accept the emotions in their entirety, the "extra" evaporates, and love remains.

At this stage, we will add the cleansing of the chakra by means of guided imagining to the linking-up meditation. We can use this technique for all of the chakras when we feel the need for it. Another example of cleansing the chakra in a similar way will be presented in the meditation for cleansing the heart chakra.

Free up a half-hour in which you will not be disturbed under any circumstances. Perform the meditation in a quiet and well-ventilated room, and set up an essential oil burner containing one of the aromatic oils that is suitable for the balancing, stimulation or soothing of the solar plexus chakra.

Lie down comfortably. If you tend to fall asleep, you can perform the meditation sitting up. Sit comfortably, with a straight back, without crossing your arms or legs. Begin to take slow and deep abdominal breaths and relax your entire body. Let yourself calm down. After you feel relaxed and calm, concentrate on the solar plexus chakra.

Close your eyes and visualize the solar plexus chakra as a lotus flower blooming in a yellow circle or spiral. Now, as in the previous meditations for opening the base and sex chakras, concentrate on the chakra's petals and notice whether all or some of them are open. Look at the yellow color of the chakra while you open the petals that are still closed, using the power of your imagination and making the bright, clean yellow color flow in order to reinforce the color of the chakra.

Open the petals one by one to the best of your ability. Now, with your eyes still closed, see your image in your imagination becoming smaller until it is small enough to enter the chakra region that is located in the diaphragm area. Stand in the center of the chakra. There may be spots –

brown, gray, black – in the yellow of the chakra. The color may be slightly faded or have a dust-like texture. See yourself standing in the center of the chakra, the petals open (completely or partially) around you. Look around. Find a bucket of water, a watering can, a mop, a broom, or anything else your imagination can provide you for cleaning the chakra. Those spots are traumas of the ego, anger, non-positive feelings, guilt feelings and other such emotional baggage. Take the cleaning utensil you imagined and start to clean the spots you noticed in the chakra. You will certainly notice that when you perform the "cleaning action," the spots actually disappear. The spots and "dirt" that are simply impressions remaining from painful or inhibiting emotions disappear easily. This can attest to the fact that you have already done profound mental or spiritual work on this topic, and therefore cleaning the remaining impression is fast and easy.

Spots or dirt that originate in situations with which you have not yet made your peace may require more work. If you come across a spot that reappears after you have cleaned it, concentrate on it. Concentrate on the feeling that arises in you when you look at it or feel it. At this point, a certain situation, picture, feeling or even event may rise up clearly in front of your eyes. You have the capacity to repair, complete and create a situation of peace with this situation and these feelings here and now. Let yourself feel the feeling, think about the particular person (if the matter is connected with a particular person), or see the picture. Let yourself understand the emotions that rise up inside you. Is it fear? Fear of what? Anger? Jealousy? Don't be afraid of discovering the source of the "spot" on the chakra. Even if it is a difficult and painful event, you are the one who chose to undergo this experience in order to grow and bloom. Now it's time to make peace with it. Send love to the event, person or situation the spot on the chakra represents. Pay attention to whether this energetic burden is yours. Ask yourself this question while concentrating on the picture or the feeling that the spot evokes in you or on the picture that rises up in front of your eyes. This may be an energetic burden that does not belong to you, but you have chosen to take it upon yourself for some reason. If that is the situation, tell yourself: "I am responsible for myself only." If you know from whom you received or took this pain or burden, send him love.

Now, thank the state or feeling represented by the spot. Thank it for helping you know who you are *not* – you are not the anger, the sadness, the guilt or any other negative emotion represented by the spot. You only experience it in order to know what is not a part of your being and your soul. Accept those emotions as "teachers" who teach you who you are *not* in order to discover who you *are*. If this energetic burden does not belong to you, thank it and send it back to the source.

"An energetic burden that does not belong to you" refers to the problems of other people that you have taken upon yourself because of a feeling of responsibility, identification, guilt, and so on, or that were given to you verbally or physically. (For instance, take a situation of a mother or a father hitting the child – they are "giving" him the energetic burden of their own anger. This is also true for verbal accusations, demands, conditions laid down by the people close to you – "I will love you if you are such-and-such, if you do such-and-such," and so on.)

Now, make glowing, clean and pure yellow light flow into the chakra. You can see it descending from above, from the source, from infinity, and penetrating your head, going down the spine, filling your body, and enveloping the chakra. The yellow light "completes" your cleaning work. The cleaning work created a situation in which you relinquished many things that are not "you" – emotions, feelings or inhibiting and blocked situations. When these have been "cleaned" and removed, your ability to accept is greater, and you are ready to regain your personal strength, strength that you yourself may have relinquished to other people. Relinquishing strength to other people is reflected in many different ways. It can be seen, for instance, when relinquishing personal responsibility and handing it to a guru, a religious functionary, a friend, a mate, a parent or anyone else – in this or another incarnation – toward whom you have nurtured some kind of expectations. Expecting anything of the other person causes us to give him our strength, since we depend on him for our continued activity or our feelings, and give him the right to influence them or navigate them, instead of us being our own navigators, creating and operating our reality and all of our feelings. Of course, anger toward others, accusing others, making demands of others and laying down conditions for others are also forms of relinquishing our strength into their hands, whether they want it or not. Now, after the cleansing, while you are filling the chakra with reviving yellow light, ask for your strength back. Tell the universe that you are one of its expressions (actually you are declaring this to yourself to the same extent as you are saying it to the universe) – "I am prepared to receive my strength back. I accept my strength back."

Let yourself feel the marvelous feeling of your strength, which was always yours, coming back and becoming a part of you. Continue inhaling yellow light until you feel replete. Continue taking deep breaths and surrendering yourself to this pleasant feeling for a few more minutes, as you feel fit.

After you have completed the meditation, write down the experiences that emerged in your notebook or commit them to memory. Since the awareness of your ability to cleanse and liberate yourself of emotions that inhibit the action of the solar plexus chakra and create barriers in it (just like cleansing the other chakras of various residues) does not disappear after the meditation, various experiences may emerge in your consciousness for a few days following the meditation. It is a good idea to perform a similar process to the one you performed while meditating – recognition, cleansing, sending everything that does not belong to you back to the source, calling on your strength to come back to you, and accepting it.

The fourth chakra

The heart chakra

Anahatra

❁ CHAKRAS ❁

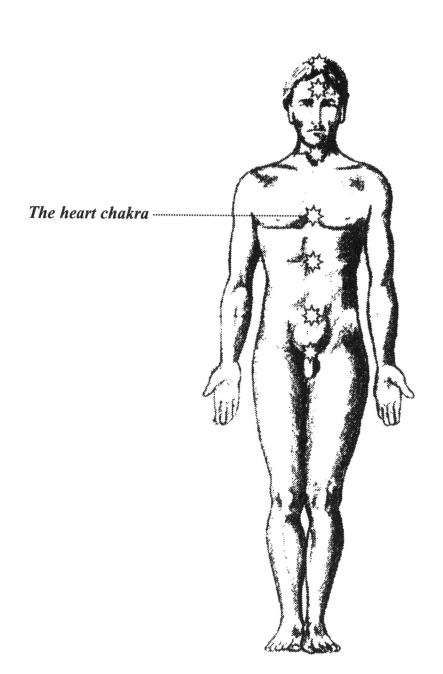

The heart chakra ···············

Location of the chakra: Parallel to the heart, in the center of the body.

Colors: Green and pink.

Complementary color: Magenta.

Symbol: A circle surrounded by 12 lotus petals, and inside it a six-pointed star containing the letters of the sound "yam." The chakra's stem emerges from the six-pointed star. Another symbolic element attributed to this chakra is gray-green smoke.

Key words: Emotion, compassion, softness, love, balance.

Basic principles: Devotion.

Inner aspect: Love.

Energy: Harmony.

Age of development: 13 or 14 to 15 years.

Element: Air.

Sense: Touch.

Sound: "Yam."

Body: The feeling body.

Nerve plexus: The tactile nerves, such as the nerves in the fingertips that transmit the sensation of touch. (However, some people claim that the heart chakra is not connected to any nerve plexus.)

Hormonal glands linked to the chakra: The thymus gland.

Body organs linked to the chakra: The heart, the circulatory system, the lungs, the immune system, the thymus gland, the upper back, the skin, and the hands.

Problems and diseases that occur during an imbalance of the chakra: Respiratory problems, cardiac pains, heart attacks, hypertension, tension, anger, a non-positive attitude toward life, insomnia, fatigue.

Essential oils: Sandalwood, rose, cedarwood.

Crystals and stones: Aventurine, chrysocolla, rose quartz, emerald, jade, chrysoprase, dioptase, malachite, rhodonite.

Stars and astrological signs linked to the chakra: The heart chakra is symbolized by the planets Venus, Saturn (since it symbolizes overcoming personal ego and striving toward unconditional love), and the sun, and by the signs Libra, Leo, and Sagittarius.

Libra, which is dominated by Venus, symbolizes the aspiration to balance and harmony, contact, love, and personal development.

Leo, which is dominated by the sun, symbolizes emotional warmth, generosity, and honesty.

Sagittarius, which is dominated by Jupiter, symbolizes abundance, growth, and expansion, wisdom and experience.

The meaning of the chakra's name in Sanskrit, Anahatra, is "the ever-beating drum." The chakra is located in the center of the chest, parallel to the heart, and it connects the three lower chakras to the three upper chakras. As a result, it constitutes the "heart" of the entire chakra system. It joins the physical and emotional centers to the centers of high mental activity, and to the spiritual centers.

The six-pointed star, which is located in the center of the chakra's symbol, symbolizes the link between upper and lower, and the meeting point between these two triangles – the upper chakras and the lower chakras – which is the heart chakra.

The heart chakra is the center for love, empathy, caring about others, giving, devotion, and, consequently, the ability to heal. Thanks to its action, we are able to tune into the other, "feel" him, touch him, and let him touch us – emotionally, spiritually, and physically. The ability to connect to the other enables us to link up to the entire universe and to the divine force. Via this chakra, we feel the beauties of nature and the harmony inherent in it, and aspire to this harmony in all levels of our lives. Because of this aspiration to harmony, the chakra arouses in us the desire to feel the harmony that reigns in the different arts – music, painting, etc. – arts whose very existence stimulates and opens our hearts. This is the center in which words, sounds, and scenes are converted into feelings and emotion.

The heart chakra is located between the solar plexus chakra, which is the center for the basic emotions, and the throat chakra, which is the center for self-expression, and it is via the heart chakra that the basic emotions (from the solar plexus chakra) are purified in preparation to express personal power (in the throat chakra).

Thanks to the heart chakra, we can love and aspire to love. It directs our ability to give, to bestow, and to receive love, and it aspires to attain the ability to bestow unconditional, ego-free, and disinterested love, as well as openness to divine love. The aspiration to unity on all levels derives from it: from physical and tangible unity through love for one's mate to unity that stems from the love of nature and the universe. It also stimulates the ability to open up to celestial love and faith, which come from the fifth energy center, the throat chakra. Without opening the heart chakra, faith cannot be complete. The true aspiration is to unconditional love.

When the chakra is fully open and balanced, this kind of love, which is expressed for the sake of pure love only, cannot "get lost," nor is there any need or desire to "guard" it. When the chakra is not altogether open and balanced (which is very common), we experience fears of abandonment, fear of loss of love, and the misery of rejection. Unconditional love can never be rejected or forced.

When it is connected to the action of the upper chakras, this love becomes love of God and a feeling of the celestial power in every atom and component of creation. From this insight, the person sees the beauty and the divine in every person and creature, and can connect to the good and positive in it.

The heart chakra is also responsible for self-love, just as the solar plexus chakra is responsible for self-esteem. Without true self-love and acceptance, it is not possible to love the other entirely. The saying, "love thy neighbor as thyself" tells us that we have to love ourselves in order to be able to love our neighbor. When self-love is not complete, we discover our own flaws in every other person as a result of a lack of awareness. The people who come into our lives frequently act as a mirror for our own personality, and when we do not accept our character traits, it is exactly those properties – directly, conversely, or indirectly – that will anger or bother us in others.

For this reason, on the way to acquiring the ability to connect to the force of the universe, our hearts have to learn how to love and accept ourselves and others.

From the heart chakra, we learn how to give of ourselves, forgive, excuse, and pity. Compassion is the ability to "feel the other," to empathize with his pain and sorrow with understanding and without judging him. The expression, "putting oneself into someone else's shoes" explains the essence of compassion. When we judge a person who is experiencing a problem, pain, or sorrow, true compassion cannot be realized inside us. Since we are not in his shoes, we do not know the burden of his present life or past lives. Man sees the exterior, while God looks inside us. The external appearance is often deceptive, and judgment prevents us from opening our hearts to love and empathy.

The basic emotions in the sexual chakra, which are activated in relation to the "I" in the solar plexus chakra, become conscious emotions in the heart chakra. In the solar plexus chakra, working on our emotions and acknowledging them leads to self-awareness and an increase in inner strength, while the wisdom that joins those aspects in the heart chakra opens them up to feeling the rest of humanity, and makes them less focused on the "I." When we open our hearts, we permit ourselves to be sensitive, and to expose our inner side and our softness. Softness is not only expressed in touch, but in the entire being. Steadfast self-knowledge and acknowledged inner strength are necessary in order for us to allow ourselves to be soft and emotionally exposed. However, this exposure enables us to be in constant touch with our own and other people's emotions, to receive love, and to remove the masks that we use to protect our soft inner side. When the solar plexus chakra is balanced, and the inner strength is aware and expresses itself properly, the heart chakra can permit the openness that leads to softness and acceptance. We feel strong enough to behave with softness and compassion toward the other, without the need to be constantly on the defensive, and wear protective "armor" in our relationships with those around us.

When the heart chakra is open and balanced, we feel inner faith. We understand that the power of God means love for every life form, and we are led to the higher function of the chakra, which is the ability to love not only those who are close to us, or human beings, but the entire universe.

The heart chakra is also responsible for another aspect of the deep empathy toward which it is directed in a balanced state: the ability to keep the "I" intact, and not identify with the other so much that the self is swallowed up, nor does it allow the pains of the other to filter into the "self." This aspect is important for everyone – especially for therapists. Even when we are prepared to help a person with our entire being – to give of ourselves with no intention of being rewarded and without any other self-interest, the same cut-off point is necessary for the integrity and health of the self. Over-identification can be a sign that the heart chakra is not properly balanced. When the person "drowns" in another person's troubles to the point that they disrupt his basic equilibrium, or affect his functioning, his reward turns into loss. In order to give, the person has to maintain a solid and connected center that is not swept away in the other person's torrent of pain and problems. There is a need for the ability to distance oneself in order to gain the objectivity that enables the person to see things in proportion, thus giving the other person the assistance he really needs. The ability to detach oneself and see things from the side, even if one feels genuine involvement and a sincere desire to help and to bestow love and compassion, also comes from the energetic activities of the heart chakra.

The chakra's age of development

The heart chakra's age of development is between the ages of 13-14 and 15, approximately. At this age, the person tends to be sensitive and fragile, and reacts fully to the external world. In parallel, he becomes more aware of the processes occurring within him. At this age, he is already required to "give" to his immediate surroundings. He is expected to understand, to participate, to care – and he is at the delicate age at which he is turning from a child into a youth.

Those are also the ages at which first love is experienced, immature but deep, and sometimes it is experienced extremely intensely. The youngster still greatly needs his parents' support, but demands (or takes) greater freedom of action and of opinion, seeks to discover new experiences, and displays a greater interest in what is going on in the world. At this age, the young person begins to feel himself more as a part of society or the community, and not just as a part of the limited family unit. Certain opinions are formed, fields of interest broaden, and the obligation to contribute to society – sometimes still in the limited family setting – expands and becomes more significant.

At this age, the young person wants a greater range of action, more freedom. This is when the trust between him and his parents comes into play. The youngster has his own wishes and experiences a need to feel that his parents respect him. However, he still seeks and needs certain limits to mark out a path and prevent him from making mistakes that can harm him. He may lack confidence about what he really wants, and conversely, obstinately stick to his opinion because of his demand for the freedom he feels he deserves.

Another conflict that is liable to occur at this age is the "surprising" discovery that his parents are not perfect. The more the parent insists on sticking to his guns without providing logical explanations that satisfy the adolescent, the more the latter's urge to rebel that characterizes this age is aroused. He is now more aware and mature, and notices what goes on in other family units very much. He observes his parents' mistakes or their helplessness in certain cases, and sometimes feels unconscious anger that they are not as perfect as he perceived them when he was a child. He compares and checks, and may address complaints to them. Having said that, the rebellious stage is natural and even healthy. At this stage, the youngster wants to create his self-image, separate from the family unit, which he still needs. He wants to define who and what he is and sever the umbilical cord in order to feel more independent. This stage is essential, since the adolescent must prepare himself for life as a mature and independent person with his own paths, opinions and lifestyle. While he is discovering himself, his desires and his aspirations, he may find himself caught in an inner conflict, when those opinions are very different than his parents' opinions and lifestyle. Sometimes, for the sake of self-definition, the adolescent feels a need to "shatter" the conventions accepted by his parents, and define them as "conservative." This situation is liable to lead to serious conflicts in the home on the one hand and self-effacement of the adolescent on the other, when he represses his inner opinions and beliefs for fear of those conflicts. It is a fine line, and frequently the parents find that they are helpless and do not know how to cope with the situation. However, it can also be a wonderful period in which the parents discover their child's nascent personality in all its glory.

A situation in which the parents respect their adolescent child's opinions and wishes, but also explain to him in an enlightened way why they believe in certain values and why they behave as they do, can reinforce the ties between parent and child, and create profound mutual esteem. In contrast, when the adolescent feels that his parents despise and are ashamed of his behavior, which he sees as a part of his character and of his image and cannot find anything reprehensible about it, he is caused a great deal of suffering. During this period, the parents must form an objective and considered opinion that will enable them to set clear priorities. For instance, when the parent reacts with anger or rejection to the way the youngster dresses, even though it is harmless, or imposes various prohibitions and limitations that are superfluous, a situation is created in which the adolescent loses his faith in his parents and then, when it is necessary for them to veto something that really is liable to harm him, the adolescent may not understand the significance of the prohibition, and may view it as simply "something else that Mom and Dad object to."

While his personality is forming and he is beginning to define himself consciously, the adolescent is in great need of encouragement. His external appearance, like his personal expectations in his studies, can be profoundly influenced by his parents' attitude toward him. A suitably healthy attitude, which accepts the youth as he is, without demanding more than he is capable of at a given time, as well as respect for his external appearance, his image and his personality, help him form healthy self-esteem.

At these ages, some parents feel that the youngster is drifting away from them. Certain parents tend to react to this natural distancing with deep inner fear. When the heart chakra is damaged in the parent (something that is very common in this context, especially with mothers), the parent is liable to fear his child's distancing himself from him, even though it is completely natural. This kind of suffocating love is one of the causes for the development of physical problems such as allergies and asthma. These problems may occur in the youngster at a very early age, but are activated during adolescence as a consequence of the "suffocating love" that is lavished on him by the parent, who is constantly worried about him and sends him messages expressing trepidation and a lack of confidence.

Harmonious functioning of the heart chakra

When the heart chakra is balanced, it has a beneficial influence on all the other chakras. The heart chakra links them together, since it is located between the upper three and the lower three chakras. When the chakra is balanced, it operates in harmony with the other chakras by helping the person become a channel that receives divine love and causes it to flow. The chakra's outward radiation onto the rest of humanity and the universe is tremendous. The activity of the properly-balanced heart chakra, especially when that balance exists in the other chakras as well, grants the person enormous power of love, which flows abundantly, consciously and unconsciously, over the people around him. This state creates a person who is sought after and pleasant to be with, because his presence is soothing, consoling, and supportive. The person feels connected to other people, and empathetic and understanding toward them. He feels a powerful connection with those around him – but is nonetheless in tune with himself and emotionally stable. He himself feels happy and self-confident, and his presence inspires similar feelings in the people around him. In his company, they feel free, uncensured, and able to open their hearts easily. People whose heart chakra is open and balanced occasionally get reactions such as "You've helped me so much!" or "This talk with you has really helped me!" when in fact they hardly said anything – they just listened with understanding and affection! It is very easy to "spill one's guts" to such a person, and to feel that one has been given help and genuine relief, even if the person did not help actively or offer advice. Just being around a person whose heart chakra is open and balanced is truly "infectious." The energetic interaction causes the people around him "to open up their hearts," so that the person feels as if he himself has been given affection and understanding by people he knows as well as from strangers. This creates a pleasant and harmonious life in which the person encounters smiling faces and the desire to help wherever he goes (even from strangers in unfamiliar places), since the effect of an open and balanced heart chakra on the surroundings is enormous, and attracts love to its owner.

When the chakra is open and balanced, the person feels a desire to help, and an ability to be empathetic, and this is absolutely natural. Having said that, when the chakra is fully balanced, energy cannot be "sucked" from him, nor can he be exhausted or his good will exploited. He himself is aware of what he can give and knows his inner limits. The help he gives others does not serve to satisfy his ego or to make him feel superior to the person he is helping – rather, it is natural and flowing. A person whose heart chakra is open and balanced may offer assistance that is not exactly what the asker had in mind, but it is the appropriate and correct assistance, because the person can remain objective and discern what the other person really needs.

From the emotional point of view, an open and balanced heart chakra causes the person to accept his emotions totally naturally, without conflicts or a lack of confidence in them. He is not afraid of expressing his feelings, nor is he shocked by other people expressing theirs to him – by crying, cheerfulness, exuding warmth, and so on – since they are absolutely natural. Because he is able to accept his own feelings, he is blessed with the ability to accept and understand other people's. He considers the feelings legitimate and positive, and he will encourage the people to express them, not to repress them. The more balanced the rest of the chakras, with no inhibiting spiritual or psychological factors, the more pleasant it becomes to be in the company of the person with the open heart chakra. Of course, this affects his family and social relationships, and creates harmony wherever he goes.

As we said previously, the effect of an open and balanced heart chakra on the surroundings is tremendous. The fact that the chakra's energy flows freely creates an interaction with other people's heart chakras, and even people who are blocked and "hard-hearted" soften and reveal the love that is deep inside them on one level or another. The energies involved in the interaction with the soft and non-judgmental energies of love and compassion of the person with the open heart chakra can cause the hearts of hard people to melt and their anger to be assuaged and calmed. This is because their own heart chakra wants to be balanced (like the person whose heart chakra exudes warmth and love). In order to see how this situation works in practice, we can look at a familiar example: There is a car accident, and the two drivers pull up at the side and get out of their cars. One of them is red in the face, furious, fuming, and accusatory, even if the accident was his fault. The other, in contrast, is serene and relaxed, and forestalls the first one's yells by asking forgiveness sincerely, by apologizing in a respectful and empathetic manner, and by inquiring sincerely about the first one's physical wellbeing and the state of his car. It is often possible to see how the furious person, who occasionally uses attack as a form of defense so as to avoid blame, swallows his anger in surprise, calms down, and allows the person with the balanced heart chakra to involve him in a civilized conversation that is beneficial to both parties.

Self-love and acceptance, and love for other people, which become an inherent part of the life of the person with the open and balanced heart chakra, cause him to aspire to divine love – universal love. As a result, the person is aware of the laws of the universe, and operates naturally according to the cosmic dictum of "love thy neighbor as thyself". He understands that the sadness and suffering on earth originate in the separation from and inattention to the divine part of ourselves – to our soul. He aspires to connect, and understands that the initial separation was necessary in order to connect, just like death exists so that regeneration and vitality can occur. His will to live and his joy of life increase, and the world looks beautiful and welcoming. The person does not merely "live for himself," distanced from what is going on in the world around him, but rather feels at one with the rest of the creatures of the universe – human beings, members of the plant and animal kingdoms, the earth, and the celestial forces. His understanding of the laws of the universe enables him to view his personal experiences in a new light. Because of his correct emotional and mental interpretation of these events, he experiences certain situations – that may be traumatic or painful to other people – in a more understanding, profound, and tranquil way.

Unharmonious functioning of the heart chakra

Unharmonious functioning of the heart chakra is expressed in the various aspects of the person's ability to give and take. This state is liable to be manifested in a feeling that the person can give love, support, and help, but in fact he is not connected to the genuine nourishing and fulfilling source of love. Of course, this may cause mental exhaustion as a result of the person giving love when he is unable to accept love. He feels uncomfortable with displays of affection, and prefers to define himself as "a person who doesn't need others," since he interprets support, assistance, and accepting affection as weakness, and, in parallel, his giving can never be totally whole. This state is clearly expressed in various relationships, too. On the energetic level, however, it is likely to cause the person to feel unable to accept love, or feel unconsciously that he is not worthy of love. Accordingly, he does not attract or invite love to himself in the energetic layer. This situation is evident in all aspects of life. The more the person tries to convince himself consciously or unconsciously that he does not need love, the less love he will receive. This sometimes stems from experiences of rejection of love during adolescence, when parents tend to classify their child as too "big" for concrete, physical love. In this way, he learns to repress his need for love, and later on finds it difficult to accept love and displays of affection even from his mate.

Another situation that arises from the lack of balance between giving and receiving is the situation in which the person bestows, and lavishes warmth and love on his surroundings without being aware of the need to keep his center stable and balanced. He is emotionally blackmailed, in a state of constant giving, and feels that this is not reciprocated. We must remember that when the chakra is balanced, the person does not give in order to receive. He gives naturally and openly, and does not feel the need to get something in return, because the fact of giving is what is important to him. When the chakra is not balanced, the person feels a need deep in his heart to get something in return for what he has given. If he does not get anything, he feels disappointed and used and sometimes even bitter. When there is an imbalance in the heart chakra, the person's giving and affection may simply be a way of receiving affirmation, consent, or affection from other people. He fears rejection, and is afraid that if he stands up for himself, gives to himself, and concentrates on himself (when necessary), he will be defined as an "egoist" or will be rejected in some way. It is difficult for him to find the place in which self-love and love for others become one universal love, and feels that these two things are in perpetual conflict.

The colors of the chakra

The colors of the heart chakra are green and pink. Green is the color that is located between the warm and the cold colors, and is neither warm nor cold, but balancing. It is considered to be the general color of health, and represents harmony, balance, youth, freshness, growth, energy and hope. It is an extremely powerful balancing color, and has an emotional and physical balancing action. It soothes, strengthens, and stimulates vitality, growth, harmony and the ability to overcome obstacles and take a new path. Because of its capacity to balance energies and restore harmony, it is helpful in attaining a new and healthful physical and mental structure. Since it is one of the dominant colors in the plant kingdom, it symbolizes the harmonious cyclical character of nature, the laws of nature, and growth and renewal.

Green is the color of physical health. It is used for treating every problem barring cancer. (Since it encourages growth, there are people who claim that it is liable to accelerate the growth of existent malignant tumors.) It exerts a significant effect on the emotional state because it stimulates the pituitary gland, which is the gland responsible for most of the body's hormonal functions. By stimulating it, the color green helps to balance the entire hormonal system and is effective in balancing and calming states of emotional imbalance. It has a soothing effect on the sympathetic nervous system, and is therefore effective as an analgesic. Green is the color of nitrogen, an element that constitutes 78 percent of the atmosphere and is essential for the creation of bones, muscles, and the other tissues. It helps in the treatment of muscles and bones, and is linked to the action of the muscles, bones, bronchial tubes and lungs. It exerts a beneficial effect on the organs governed by the heart chakra, and is effective in the treatment of cardiac problems and problems of the circulatory system. It has a stimulating effect on the blood vessels, and helps to balance blood pressure. It encourages cell renewal and the general regeneration of the organism, and strengthens the body in general (especially after illness or injury) by enhancing the absorption of oxygen in the body.

When the action of the heart chakra is balanced, and the chakra is open, the color green will appear balanced, bright and clean around the chakra and in the aura. In this case, the green color of the balanced chakra symbolizes the unity and balance of body, mind and spirit, an ability to display empathy and compassion, an ability to accept things as they are by understanding the laws of the universe, an ability to link up to nature and feel it, openness to accepting and giving, a feeling of love toward other people and the universe, hope, growth, transformation and re-creation, good communication and universal love. When we want to balance the chakra and develop these abilities in a person, we project the color green.

When the heart chakra is not balanced, the color green appears faded, cloudy or unharmonious. In this situation, it may attest to difficulties in accepting and giving love, a non-positive attitude toward life, pessimism, dissatisfaction, as well as jealousy, envy, a false attitude, over-sentimentality, and an inability to achieve a profound understanding of the course of life and the laws of the universe.

Occasionally, we can discern a green-yellow color around the chakra and in the entire aura. We can also project it in order to take advantage of the properties that this color symbolizes: freshness, youth, renewal and enthusiasm. It stimulates, and when it appears around the chakra or among the colors of the aura, it attests to compassion, a profound ability to forgive, sincerity, sympathy toward other people, good communication, and a love of peace.

Dark green symbolizes a good ability to present oneself, stability and a need for stability, vitality, and a good expressive ability. When it appears in the aura or around the chakra in an unbalanced and unharmonious manner, it is liable to attest to a materialistic person, one who needs concrete stability in the extreme, or whose characteristics are dominated by cunning and the capacity to defraud others.

The second color that symbolizes the heart chakra and is used for treating, balancing and opening it, is pink. Because of the presence of the red component in this color, it should not be projected onto irascible people who have a tendency toward agitation. It is excellent for treating conditions of insufficient chakra functioning, when the person feels that he does not receive love, is lonely or rejected, and also when a low level of "self-love" is detected. Because it is composed of red and white, pink connects the properties of red, which symbolizes passion and warmth, to white, which consists of all the colors of the spectrum and symbolizes divine light. For this reason, pink constitutes the color of universal love, cosmic love. It has a profound effect on the mind, soothes overexcited states, raises the body's vibrations, stimulates affections, love and the will to give, a feeling of warmth and mental protection, and helps to rejuvenate. Pink, with its soft and delicate energies, releases tension from the heart chakra, and, like green, helps treat the heart (especially when it is clear that the physical problems are connected almost consciously to emotional states) and helps to regulate blood pressure. It stimulates emotions of love and softness, creative activity and a feeling of happiness and warm cheerfulness. When we see a dominant, clear and balanced pink among the colors of the aura, it attests to great sensitivity, femininity, softness and emotionality, and in certain cases may also indicate over-sentimentality (when it is overly dominant or appears slightly unbalanced).

The connection between the heart chakra and the physical body

The heart chakra is responsible for the heart, the circulatory system, the lungs, the immune system, the thymus gland, the upper back, the skin, and the hands.

Despite the scientific claim that negates the supposition that we "feel" with our heart, the action of the heart is powerfully linked to the emotions we experience. Specific states of anger and irritation cause our blood pressure to rise, and when these states continue and recur, the condition can become permanent hypertension. When we experience loss, pain, or sorrow, the feeling of pain and emptiness often occurs in the chest, and when we experience relief from worry, we feel as if "a weight has been lifted from our heart." The heart is the organ that symbolizes the center of love and confidence: love for others and for oneself, confidence in oneself and in the universe. Ongoing emotional problems, worry that stems from a lack of confidence in the processes of the universe, and hurt resulting from love are experienced as severe traumas – all of them can be shown to be the emotional layer that is parallel to physical heart problems. Rigidity, hardness of the heart, a lack of caring, and ignoring the dictates of the heart in order to acquire money, power, and property are often shown to be the emotional layer that leads to a heart attack – or "cardiac infarction" in medical jargon. Hardening our heart toward our personal emotions and desires in order to receive society's affirmation of our existence can cause heart problems. The heart pumps the blood in our arteries and veins, and revives all the organs in our body. The life-giving blood represents the joy that flows in the body. When this joy disappears as a result of the heart chakra not being open to the beauty of the universe, problems in the circulatory system may occur.

The respiratory system, too, especially the lungs, is linked to the action of the heart chakra. Breathing is the expression of our ability to inhale life, experience it fully, and exist. When there is a lack of self-love, and the person is incapable of self-esteem and true self-love, this may manifest itself in problems of the respiratory system. The air we breathe – the element that is linked to the heart chakra – expresses the ability to connect to and be a part of the universe, on the one hand, and to define our personal space on the other. Conflicts between the ability to connect to the other and define our personal space at the same time are liable to be manifested in a range of respiratory problems. Asthma, one of the characteristics of an unbalanced heart chakra, is sometimes caused by smothering love, or by a feeling of choking that stems from the person's immediate surroundings. In children, it can be viewed as a kind of inability to breathe independently because of parents who "smother" them with love. It is not rare for the asthma to "disappear" when the child grows up and leaves home to go to college or to live an independent life. Having said that, the person can move out of his parents' home and still be deeply rooted in the same smothering patterns of love, without freeing himself of them. Consequently, he continues experiencing the distress of asthma.

The influence of the chakra on hormonal activity

The endocrine gland that is linked to the heart chakra is the thymus gland. This is a flat gland with two hemispheres that is located in the upper anterior part of the chest cavity, between the sternum and the pericardium (the membranous sac that encloses the heart). It is made of lymphatic tissue and plays an important role in the maturation of the immune system in children. It seems that T-lymphocytes, which are extremely important in the immune system, learn their function from the thymus. The thymus gland is the largest in size (in proportion to the body) in the newborn infant, and from adolescence it begins to decrease in size (in proportion to the body). In fact, it is in a state of degeneration in the adult.

The practical action of the thymus gland in adults is still a mystery. Despite huge progress in medical science, the exact action of the thymus gland in the adult human is still not known, but what is known is that its action up to adolescence is of crucial importance. It is a part of the lymphatic system, and up to the ages of 12 to 15, it secretes a hormone called the thymic humoral factor. It is possible that the gland is linked to the growth process, and to the person's progress from childhood to adulthood. Until the immune system is fully mature, the action of the thymus gland is absolutely essential. Even after that, it may still affect and stimulate the action of the immune system.

Meditations

The forgiveness meditation

Forgiveness is tremendous power. The power of forgiveness is one of the sacred mechanisms found in the heart chakra. There is no need to give reasons for forgiveness – it is our natural state, since any other state is to our disadvantage. It makes no difference what the "other person" did to us. What matters is what we keep on "doing" to ourselves – harming, hurting, and continuing to invite painful experiences because of not forgiving. Anger and resentment harm us – sometimes more than the original deed itself. More than that. When we take responsibility for our lives, and are aware of the fact that everything that happens in our world is our choice – perhaps not a conscious choice at the time of the occurrence, but nevertheless our choice – we create the "script," the event, in one way or another, and when it happens, we find ourselves surprised and angry, blaming our surroundings instead of looking inward and examining how exactly we caused it to happen. Almost certainly we did not cause it to happen physically (since in that case, we would blame ourselves), but rather by means of the thought, belief and emotional patterns we espoused, inhibiting patterns that caused us to invite non-supportive experiences into our lives and that became realities that were expressed by other people or certain situations.

Thus, the nature of forgiveness is inner forgiveness and accepting the experience as an experience, as learning, even if it was a blatantly unpleasant one.

To this end, we must relinquish the anger and resentment we feel toward the person who was involved in this experience – perhaps on the "other" side of the fence – as a harmful and painful factor.

In order to perform the meditation, free up a half-hour during which you will not be disturbed. You can perform it seated or lying down, but if you tend to fall asleep easily, you would be better off doing it sitting comfortably. Place a few drops of lavender oil in an essential oil burner in the room (preferably about a half-hour prior to the beginning of the meditation, in order to let the fragrance permeate the room). You can play gentle, quiet and pleasant music without lyrics. Spend a few minutes evoking a past event concerning a person (close to you or not) who you feel hurt you – an event that still rankles and bothers you. It could be an event that occurred a few days ago or decades ago, or even, if you are aware of it, in a previous incarnation.

Sit comfortably, link up to the music, and let it envelop you. Inhale the pleasant vapor from the lavender oil that fills the room, and take several deep slow breaths. Close your eyes. Continue breathing while healing your body. When you feel tranquil and calm, visualize a theater auditorium. See yourself sitting in one of the rows, looking at the stage. Suddenly, the image of the person with whom you want to perform the forgiveness process appears on the stage. He has not yet noticed you, so you can observe him. Look at his face, and feel the inner processes that are occurring while you are looking at him. Pay attention to your body. Notice if your muscles, especially your facial muscles, contract with anger or some other emotion. Relax them. Still looking at the person, imagine that you are inhaling pink light and exhaling green light. The pink and green lights envelop you lovingly, giving you a feeling of power and compassion. While you are looking at the person, you can begin to speak to him. Tell him what is in your heart. You may receive a response. Perhaps it will satisfy you, perhaps not. Regardless of the response – because this process is for you (the other person will have to solve his own problems himself; this is not the time, nor is there any need, to begin to teach him how to live his life or how to relate to other people – that is his lesson in life, and he has to learn it by himself), tell him that you forgive him. In your mind's eye, see his face softening and smiling.

At this point, you may feel a certain degree of relief, and you may feel that your forgiveness really comes from your heart. If not, evoke the event itself in front of your eyes – that same event that hurt you. Now, with the help of your imagination, alter it so that you feel at one with it. Feel completely free to alter the events as you wish, so long as they lead to peace and agreement. Certain insights may emerge in you at this point. After you have altered the event, go back to the theater auditorium and repeat the forgiveness procedure with the person. You can see yourself going onto the stage, approaching him and shaking his hand. After you feel that you have completed the process, let the scenes fade and disappear. Remain seated for a few minutes until you feel ready to open your eyes.

Besides the wonderful feeling of relief that accompanies the process, you may discover that the nature of your relationship with the person, especially if you are in close contact with him and still associate with him, may change, even from the other person's side! The person may disappear from your life either abruptly or gradually, if the reciprocal learning terminated with the process. In your notebook, write down the insights that emerged during the process – and may continue to do so during the subsequent days – and glance at them occasionally in order to learn more about yourself.

Meditation for cleansing the heart

In this meditation, we will cleanse the heart chakra of the non-supportive burdens it contains. This technique can also be used for cleansing any of the other chakras, but we have chosen to describe its action on the heart chakra because it is central in this context. The meditation operates both on conscious and unconscious non-supportive feelings. It does not change the situation for us only – since there is actually no such thing as "for us only." Every emotion we cleanse of non-positive residues is projected as cleansed, pure and loving to the universe and affects our immediate surroundings and beyond. For this reason, it can cause changes for the good in the way the world relates to us. It is advisable to perform this meditation several times in order to cleanse more and more residues that do not support us and turn them into love. Moreover, it is most advisable to perform it every time we experience a strong emotion.

In order to perform the meditation, you need a large or medium-size transparent quartz crystal, preferably a six-sided generator that can stand on the table. If you want to perform the meditation on the base or crown chakras, you can use a medium-size smoky quartz generator. Similarly, you can use green or pink quartz (rose quartz) for the meditation for cleansing the heart chakra, and blue quartz for cleansing the throat chakra. In principle, transparent quartz is suitable for cleansing all the chakras.

It is important to purify the crystal thoroughly before using it (by placing it in a bowl of water and sea salt for a while or, as an emergency treatment, for 15 minutes to one hour in the freezer compartment). After that, it must be charged using sunlight and moonlight or any other method you want to use. Prior to the meditation, the crystal is programmed with the aim of the meditation: to reflect back to you the fact that you are a perfect, whole and loved creature, and to stimulate self-love and self-esteem on all levels, at the same time releasing every feeling or emotion that does not support you.

Perform the meditation in a well-ventilated room that is free of energies and has a pleasant atmosphere. As we said before, it is a good idea to use a crystal that you can stand on a table opposite you. Sit on a comfortable chair in front of the table. Free up about 20 minutes for the meditation and light an essential oil burner containing one or two of the aromatic oils that are suitable for treating the heart chakra.

Place the crystal on the table in front of you so that you can gaze at it effortlessly. Begin to relax your whole body, one organ at a time, breathing consciously. Feel how you are becoming more and more relaxed and calm with each breath. Empty your mind of all thoughts and begin to gaze at the crystal. Gaze at it for a few minutes until you feel that you can see it even with your eyes closed. If it is more comfortable for you, you can continue the meditation with your eyes open.

Now, see the crystal on the table in your mind's eye. Focus your consciousness on it. Breathe consciously, taking deep and slow breaths, and see the crystal begin to grow in front of your eyes. It grows with every exhalation. With every inhalation, feel yourself becoming smaller. You can see the shrinking process in your mind's eye, as if looking at yourself from the outside. The crystal keeps on growing, while you keep on shrinking. It grows until it fills almost the entire room and is much bigger than your body. Now, walk inside it. See yourself walking toward and entering the crystal. The entry into the crystal is the entry into your own heart.

Now you are inside the crystal. Look at the space in which you are standing. Look at the stunningly beautiful walls of the crystal and its internal structures. Listen carefully to your heartbeats that are flowing to you from the crystal, in the space in which you are standing. Feel the perfect harmony, the tranquillity, the peace and the infinite love in this space. Look at the walls of the crystal. In one of the walls, see a window or some kind of porthole that can be opened.

Continue looking at the walls, floor and ceiling of the crystal. In various places in it, notice spots, gray residues, and formations that look like dirt. These spots represent islands of a lack of self-acceptance, spots that show that you do not yet accept and love yourself completely.

Look around you. In one of the corners of the crystal, you will find various cleaning utensils. These should be a broom, a mop, a vacuum cleaner, a bucket of water, or any other utensil you can use for cleaning the spots or the dirt-like formations you noticed.

Breathe deeply, and as you inhale, see green light entering the point of the crystal and enveloping your shrunken image in green or pink light. In the place you are in at the moment, there is no criticism, guilt, anger or error. Every experience, deed or feeling becomes a teaching and enriching experience in this space, a loving expression that is there to teach you *who you are not* – you are not the hurt, you are not the weakness, you are not the criticism or the judgment, you are not the anger or the remorse. All those are burdens you took upon yourself out of choice in order to learn, and you are the one who can hold them and continue experiencing them – or separate from them peacefully.

Pick up your cleaning utensils. Go over to the spots and dirt and start to clean them. While you are cleaning, remember that you yourself created these spots in order to understand, learn and know, and you are the one who has decided to clean them – the power and the choice to do so are both in your hands. Clean every speck of dust, film of dirt or spot with care and devotion. Let yourself experience the feeling of relief that occurs after you have cleaned each spot, and go on to the next spot. While cleaning one spot or dirt formation, various insights, feelings or scenes may arise, informing you about this "dirt." Accept the insight with love and thank yourself for the information, thank the feeling, the event or the experience itself for helping you learn, and continue. Remember that even if you cannot say exactly what you have learned from this experience, the crux of the learning is to teach yourself what you are not, what does not support you and what you no longer need.

The more you clean the spots, the greater your feeling of relief, fullness, and the opening of your heart. Continue cleaning until all the spots have been cleaned, or as much as you can. When you have completed the cleaning, look at the interior of the crystal again. A delightful and beautiful spring of water will appear in front of you – a stream or a waterfall in which clear water flows. Rinse your hands and your utensils off in the water, and place the utensils in one of the corners of the crystal. They may disappear the moment you put them down. If you accumulated a pile of dirt while cleaning, see yourself putting the dirt into a bag and tying it up. Place the bag into the water source. As you do so, the water will suddenly expand for a second, overflow, and swallow the bag like a toilet being flushed, making it disappear completely. Afterwards, the water source will return to its natural size and abruptly disappear. Tell yourself, "I am excreting all the unwanted emotions and thoughts through my excretory organs." It is possible, of course, that they will disappear by themselves along with the cleaning utensils.

When you have completed this process, look at your shrunken image inside the crystal – the image that performed all these actions. What is the expression on its face? Almost certainly it is smiling. If not, perhaps it feels a certain degree of loss for all the non-supportive emotional burdens you discarded. If the image is not comfortable and happy, envelop it in pink or green light and say to yourself: I am lovingly releasing every experience, feeling or emotion that does not support me. Smiling, look at the window in one of the walls of the crystal. It is wide open now. Go over to the open window and look at the universe through it. It appreciates, accepts and loves your deeds, and supports you completely. It confirms your actions and contributes in its way to the creation of a new reality in your life, a reality in which the things you released and relinquished no longer exist in the process of cleaning your heart. Send a loving and grateful smile to the universe. Gaze at it and say, "I am now ready to take my strength back, I take my strength back." When you relinquished those non-supportive spots that you cleaned and disposed of during the cleaning process, you "freed up" space for receiving new, loving and supportive experiences. At that moment of purity, self-love and kindness, you can make a wish. Express your wish as a declaration. For instance, "I am experiencing health and harmony in my body and my mind," or any other wish that is important to you. After making the wish, thank the universe again and close the window, knowing that everything you did and said during this meditation is coming true in the reality of your life, and has been granted the full support of the universe.

Concentrate on your breathing and take slightly faster breaths. See the crystal gradually decreasing in size and your image growing until you both return to your normal dimensions.

Feel yourself back in your body. Feel the chair beneath you, the sensations of your body, the various background noises in the room and outside of it. Close and open your hands, move your ankles in circular movements. Slightly contract and relax your muscles, quickly but not tightly. If you still feel as if you are floating, say to yourself, "I am here right now." Open your eyes and continue sitting for a few moments, letting the pleasant feeling that surrounds you filter inside and envelop you. When you feel ready, you can stand up. Drink a glass of water, purify the crystal and charge it on a crystal colony, in sunlight and moonlight, or in any other way you charge your crystals. Then, when you feel a need to go to the bathroom, remember that you are excreting all the non-supportive emotions and feelings of which you cleansed yourself.

You can repeat this meditation frequently – each time there is a need to purify and cleanse yourself emotionally. It is a good idea to write down the experiences that occurred during the meditation in a special notebook for work on your chakras so that the insights that arose continue supporting your spiritual work.

The fifth chakra

The throat chakra

Vishadha

❈ CHAKRAS ❈

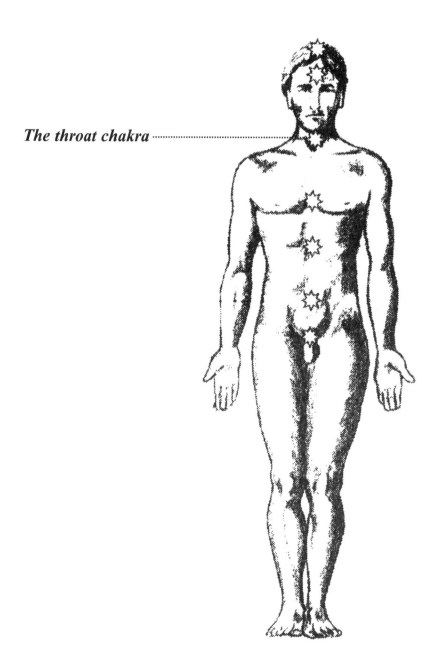

The throat chakra ·····························

Location of the chakra: The throat.

Colors: Blue, light blue, turquoise.

Complementary color: Red.

Symbol: A circle surrounded by 16 lotus petals, and inside it a circle, or a circle containing a triangle. The chakra's stem emerges from it.

Key words: Communication, expression, responsibility, universal truth, faith.

Basic principles: Nutrition, the resonance of existence.

Inner aspect: Communication and willpower.

Energy: Self-expression.

Age of development: Between 15 and 21.

Element: Ether – Akasa.

Sense: Hearing.

Sound: "Ham."

Body: The mental body.

Nerve plexus: The entire nervous system. (However, some people claim that the throat chakra is not connected to any nerve plexus.)

Hormonal glands linked to the chakra: The thyroid gland and the parathyroid glands.

Body organs linked to the chakra: The throat, the neck, the vocal cords and the vocal organs, the thyroid gland, the parathyroid glands, the jaw, the upper part of the lungs, the ears, the muscles, and the arms, and the nerves (not everyone thinks so).

Problems and diseases that occur during an imbalance of the chakra: Problems of expression, speech impediments, respiratory problems, headaches, pains in the neck, shoulders, and nape, throat problems and infections, vocal cord problems, communication problems, low self-image, a lack of creativity, emotional and thought blockages, ear infections, inflammations, and problems.

Essential oils: Lavender, patchouli.

Crystals and stones: Lapis lazuli, aquamarine, sodalite, turquoise, sapphire, blue lace agate, chrysocolla, blue tourmaline, blue quartz.

Stars and astrological signs linked to the chakra: The throat chakra is symbolized by the planets Venus, Mercury, Uranus, and Mars (which is the active planet that fulfills wishes), and the signs of Taurus, Gemini, and Aquarius.

Taurus, which is dominated by the planet Venus, symbolizes active self-expression.

Gemini is dominated by the planet Mercury, which is the planet of communication.

Aquarius, which is dominated by the planet Uranus, is the original sign of all the signs of the Zodiac.

The throat chakra's name in Sanskrit, "Vishadha," means "full of purity." It is located on the surface of the neck, in the region of the throat, with the petals on the front of the throat and the stem descending from the nape region. The throat chakra is the center for communication, inspiration, and human expression. The chakra communicates with all the aspects of communication – the self, other people, and the universal force (the communication manifests itself as faith). It joins thought and the expression of thought. This is the chakra that represents our self-image, and it creates an important link between the lower chakras and the crown chakra. It constitutes a bridge between our thoughts, our emotions, our impulses, and our reactions. Simultaneously, it transmits and expresses the contents of all the other chakras to the world. Via this chakra, we express what we are. In the previous chakras, the personality began to form, starting from the basic impulses and needs, via the unclassified basic emotions, self-definition, ego and aspirations, experiencing and classifying higher emotions – now reaching the ability to express this whole entity and present it to the world.

Via the throat chakra we express our vitality, laughter, tears, and our feelings of joy and love. This is the chakra that provides us with the ability to express consciously and clearly what operates and exists inside us.

The sexual chakra, which is linked uniquely to this chakra, is responsible for our creativity. The throat chakra supplies the inspiration. For this reason, it raises creativity to a level of artistic expression, and it is the chakra through which we release creativity into an artistic pattern – the written word (prose, poetry), music, the visual arts, dance, and so on. The passage through the chakras turns the creative energy of the sexual chakra into energy that is mixed with the desire for self-definition and expression, and then into the ability to feel and express emotion, and finally, into the ability to express creativity as an art that affects not just the creator himself, but also the spectators, listeners or readers of the work of art. This is an additional step toward the high and divine inspiration that is expressed in the third eye and crown chakras, which grant a dimension of wisdom, knowledge, and understanding of the universe to the work of art, as well as receiving divine inspiration.

The more developed the throat chakra is, the more the person can know and be aware of what is happening inside him. He is able to discern the impulses, needs, and emotions that are at work inside him, and from a certain distance, to clarify them for himself. As a result, he gains the ability to control and classify all of these inner activities, and he chooses which of them to project to the outside world, which to keep to himself, and which to release. Thus, the person has a capacity for free, objective thought, which is not affected by basic needs, or by irrelevant urges and emotions.

However, the significance of the throat chakra is not just expression, but also the ability to listen. When the person can open his ears – both the outer and the inner ears – he is able to receive profound knowledge from the universe. Listening creates tranquillity, calmness, and confidence, and together with the ability to discern objectively (that develops as a result of the chakra's action), the person can define his inner world, and discern what is happening in the external world in a clear and true way. When the inner voice is allowed to express itself, new knowledge about the "self" emerges.

The throat chakra is responsible for our self-imagination. If the solar plexus chakra expresses "what we are," this chakra expresses "what we think we are." When the chakra is open and balanced, the person is self-confident and has a positive and stable self-image that cannot be undermined. Whatever happens, he is still the same person, so he is not afraid of mistakes or failures, and they do not affect his fundamental self. The chakra's action induces a feeling of confidence and faith in higher guidance, and stimulates the person's desire to realize his cosmic vocation, which is beyond the realization of personal aspirations. From this, he aspires to self-expression that expresses all the layers of his being, which are higher than the physical and material expression.

It can be said that the throat chakra operates on two levels. On the lower level, it serves as one of the five lower chakras, and it can be linked to the basic element, senses and to the age of development. On the higher level, it is the first of the three upper chakras, and because of that it constitutes a link to the superego, to the soul, and to the spirit. When the three upper chakras are open, the person feels a true need to serve humanity. He feels that his vocation and mission in the world are linked in some way to bringing light to the world and to humanity. This feeling of vocation directs his life, in the same way in which another person is likely to lead his life according to a need to achieve obvious personal and material goals.

As a result of the chakra's dual-leveled activity, its activities can be interpreted according to both the lower layer and the upper layer.

The lower layer expresses the desire to attain satisfaction through expressing talents, desires, emotions, opinions, and so on. The person feels a need to use his voice and be heard, and to transmit his messages to those around him. On the upper level, the expression is linked to the person's spiritual qualities. It serves as an examination of self and of others, following a desire to ask new questions about the self, other people, and the world, in order to understand things in depth, and not accept them superficially and take them for granted. At this level of expression, the person is likely to use his expressive abilities – be they verbal, or the fruits of his personality or creativity – because of a desire to "give" something true, stimulating, and motivating to the rest of humanity. It is possible to see the difference between these two levels of expression very clearly in the different arts, especially the more popular arts. Today, there are many artists whose principal expression is that of their "I" and externalizing it. This action serves personal purposes – a need for recognition, self-expression, admiration from others, and so on. In contrast, there are artists who want to use their artistic ability to create a better world, increase the awareness of their audience, or provide the admirers of their works with mental and spiritual enjoyment.

The throat chakra is also the chakra that stimulates our sense of responsibility. This responsibility is expressed first and foremost in taking responsibility for oneself, for one's own development, and for one's personal life. On the higher level, this responsibility receives its meaning according to the concept of responsibility for others. This does not mean a need to interfere in or direct or control other people's lives, but rather understanding how my actions, my intentions, and my thoughts affect the world in general. On this level, the meaning of responsibility is reacting to the demands of the universe, to the superego, and to the higher goal. It expresses the ability to listen to and hear the call of the universe, which inspires the person to act for humanity and the universe, in accordance with his vocation and his path of destiny.

Communication, the essence of the throat chakra's action, can also be expressed in the lower and the higher layers. Communication is a vital need. It occurs unceasingly in the person's world – internally, as internal communication, and with the external world. The same essence of communication also occurs between our bodies, the physical body and the energetic bodies. The comprehension of this communication expresses one of the higher activities of the throat chakra.

As we said before, that same communication also occurs in the body itself, which reacts to external stimuli and internal processes. When the person is healthy, the inner physical communication and the communication between the physical body and the energetic bodies that contain the mass of emotions and thoughts, are taken for granted. In contrast, when some kind of disturbance occurs in communication – for example, when the person does not listen to his body, and pollutes it with unhealthy food or exhausts it in some way – the body reacts with unequivocal messages in order to draw the person's attention to the unbalanced state. Working with the throat chakra – opening and balancing it – leads to better and more profound communication with the physical body, and enables the person to listen to his body. To the same extent, it enables him to look objectively at the emotional and mental processes that he experiences (some of which can harm his physical, mental, and spiritual integrity), to relate to them accordingly, and fix whatever is in need of repair. This state generates a larger responsibility toward his body and soul. The person can view what is happening in his body and soul as something that falls within the realm of his personal responsibility, instead of getting involved with attributing physical and mental events to various external reasons. Examples of the latter are: "That guy annoyed me and made me angry," or "There's a flu epidemic now, and everyone's sick." He begins to look and to ask himself why these things occur, and where his personal responsibility and action lie in the framework of these events.

As we saw in the description of the link between the various chakras and the physical body, the source of every physical illness or disorder lies in a state of imbalance in one or more of the chakras, as well as in a particular thought or emotional pattern that permits the onset of the problem or the disease. When we can assume personal responsibility for our life and for our physical and mental state, as a result of the chakra's action, we can understand the way in which our patterns of thought and emotion create various physical manifestations in our world. We can understand that we get angry when we choose to get angry and suffer from states of physical disharmony when we choose to cling to inhibiting and unhealthy thought and emotional patterns. Often, when the throat chakra is blocked or unbalanced in the extreme, the person finds it difficult to understand and internalize the way in which his thoughts and emotions affect his body, as well as the physical reality in which he lives. Sometimes this conjecture appears totally false to him, and he prefers to blame his hypertension on his "annoying and pressurizing boss," and has difficulty attributing his slipped disk to something that goes beyond "I made a wrong movement." In a certain way, this is resistance to assuming personal responsibility for one's life and a lack of faith in our ability to create our physical reality and affect it.

Communication permits awareness. It clearly proves to us the power of the word, and consequently helps us understand the power of thought. Via our communication – input and output – we transmit messages and receive information. We can understand the world and things that go on in it better, and clarify our opinions, ideas, and wishes. Today's sophisticated communication system makes it quite clear that closing our eyes to what's going on in the world is no longer possible. We know what's happening in almost every corner of the world, sometimes even in real time. The reaction time that is demanded of us today is also faster, and the messages that we send to the world arrive at their destination at a tremendous speed. Our perception of the world has to be broader. We can understand and internalize the fact that different people have a different mentality and a different lifestyle to ours. Peeking at their lives by reading newspapers or surfing the Net, by watching TV or listening to the radio, and discovering how similar they are to us, reinforces their humanity.

Communicative action is so powerful that it creates the future. When we react in a certain way by saying something, we create an instantaneous or continuous future. The utterance, "Pass me the salt," creates a possible future in which the salt will be passed to me. The utterance, "Come here," creates a possible future in which you are next to me. The way we navigate our external communication navigates the realization or non-realization of future reality, as well as how it will be realized. The same goes for both external and internal communication. The things we say among ourselves, the thoughts that are realized in our mental aura, have tremendous power to create our physical reality. The saying "think before you act," clarifies the realization of our thoughts in our environmental reality. Our thought patterns, both conscious and unconscious, direct the manner of our action and conduct on the one hand, and the way the universe reacts to us on the other, by realizing what we create in our thoughts. The stronger our awareness of the power of thought is, the more we discover that thought is a powerful tool for molding reality. When we are aware of this, we refrain from thinking destructive and non-positive thought (since this invites a similar reality), and adhere to constructive and positive thought so as to create that kind of reality.

Being aware of the power of thought, and understanding that thought is active and clear energetic power, leads us to the higher type of communication of the throat chakra. The higher communicative aspect of the throat chakra is the ability to become real in our thought as a creative and active force on the one hand, and to be attentive to the laws of the universe, to the superego, and to divine messages on the other. This higher ability links the activity of the throat chakra to that of the third eye and crown chakras, and when they are open and balanced, it is even possible to channel.

One of the additional key words that describes the action of the throat chakra is universal truth. In each one of us, there is an aspiration to truth that is expressed in the lower layers of the chakra's action as law and order. Law and order create a certain truth for us, according to which we measure certain activities, live according to certain norms, and create certain criteria. By nature, the person needs a certain feeling of justice and of conscience. Our personal feelings of justice, and of conscience, are greatly influenced by social norms, and when we and our surroundings operate according to them, we feel that "everything's OK."

However, these norms are mainly the results of human thought. On the chakra's higher plane of action, we are seeking universal truth. At this stage, the social norms that define truth, law, and order, may seem imperfect to us and sometimes erroneous or unsatisfactory. However, true wisdom enables us to discover and understand the laws of the universe, and to operate according to our inner truth, conscience, and integrity, by being directed to the pure laws of the universe, without creating a clash between them and the social laws and norms. From that, we can define for ourselves more clearly what justice is, for instance, while social justice, even according to its legal criteria, is not always clear and satisfactory. We may define for ourselves what truth is – is it action that is in line with what the person says, or beyond that, is in line with his inner thoughts and his general conduct? What is peace? Is it non-war, or is it the ability to accept the other in a whole and perfect manner, out of respect and esteem? And so on. Asking these questions creates our personal uniqueness, and inspires us to go back and discover the laws of the universe and universal truth that is found, awake or asleep, in each one of us.

The chakra's age of development

The throat chakra's age of development is between the ages of 15 and 25. It is the last chakra to which significant development at certain ages can be attributed, since the next two chakras, the third eye chakra and the crown chakra, are ageless from the point of view of development.

Most conscious learning takes place at these ages, with formal learning being very important. The adolescent, having committed himself to taking responsibility for his studies, finds himself under greater pressure of exams than in previous years, and to quite a large extent, he is expected to be able to answer the question, "What do you want to do with your life?" Childhood is already behind him, and he is advancing toward adulthood.

At this age, the young person begins to be more clearly conscious of his talents. He begins to think seriously about his future and how he can combine his talents and ambitions on the one hand and his ability to live in a state of physical and mental wellbeing on the other.

In some countries, at around 17 years of age, many youngsters are on the verge of being conscripted into the army, and military service poses many conflicts for them. This is a stage in which the person must be "himself," since the influence of his parents and of the warm family unit is gradually becoming a less substantial part of his life. At these ages, the concept of responsibility becomes concrete and clear. The young person is required to "take responsibility for his life," to decide the path along which he wants to go, what he wants to achieve or realize, and how he can accomplish these objectives and achievements. Military service places a great deal of responsibility on his shoulders. He is far more responsible for himself, but is also very responsible for others, and the decisions he makes may affect those around him to a great extent.

It is also an age in which the person's awareness of what is going on around him becomes more active. The person is more involved in what is going on in the country and prepares himself to some extent for practical involvement by voting in the elections. Young people tend to form political opinions that may reflect those of their parents or conversely may be an expression of their own personal opinions. Young people of this age sometimes experience a certain feeling of mission. What is going on in the world is no longer a distant event, but rather an event that sparks involvement, and the person is keen to contribute or do something in order to improve what is going on in his world. A certain individualism may arise, and a desire to change things, which is the outcome of a growing feeling of social justice, spurs the person on to become socially involved either actively or theoretically.

At these ages, the young person's individualism, which has just formed and still evokes questions and conflicts, is put to the test. Many parents project their desire for their children to succeed – from the point of view of social status, education and economics. The social norms that define success, norms that change from one era to the next, also have a great influence on the young person. He may respond to the expectations of his parents or of society, sometimes at the expense of his inner honesty with himself, of his personal beliefs and opinions, and of his personal aspirations. This situation is liable to create a powerful breakdown in inner communication. When the young person fulfills other people's expectations, which do not match his own inner aspirations, opinions or perceptions, he is being dishonest with himself. He is then liable to begin to study for a profession that is not really what he dreamed of, to join social circles that do not really suit him, and to act according to society's expectations – "get a good job," "get a profession that's needed," "find a girl/boyfriend and get married." When the person compromises and meets these expectations at the wrong time for him or in a way that is not at one with his personal path, he is liable to suffer for many a long year.

The insight that the profession he acquired or the life he is leading are not really what he dreamed about is not easy to live with and requires immediate and drastic action. For this reason, many people repress it and live their lives in a state of constant dissatisfaction and lack of fulfillment.

The young person's inner honesty – his ability to understand himself and define what he really wants – is greatly influenced by the action of his developing throat chakra. He has to be aware of himself and understand his role in the universe in order to define his true aspirations to himself. When he cannot do this, he is liable to act according to the expectations of his family and society, and lose his personal and unique expression in life.

The young person's self-image reaches a more or less formed state that will affect the choices he will make in his adult life. Self-image, which influences and is influenced by the state of the throat chakra, can direct the person to make the life choices that suit him. When self-image is low, the young person feels unable to cope with things that, deep inside himself, he knows he can deal with. This situation creates a serious conflict. There is the deep inner knowledge of who I am , what I am capable of, and what my role in the world is. This knowledge accompanies the person throughout his entire life, but this is the age at which he begins to be aware of it. Sometimes, because of a low self-image, the person does not believe in his power to accomplish certain aims. When his immediate surroundings apply pressure, do not understand him, and are non-supportive and inappreciative, the person is liable to be compelled to cope with these conflicts, and his strength diminishes as a result.

The significance of external communication becomes extremely essential at these ages. When the person does not communicate with his immediate surroundings or with his family unit correctly, this unbalanced communication can become an established norm to which everyone becomes accustomed. Furthermore, the inability to communicate well in more distant settings – for example, when applying to an educational institution or workplace or making overtures to the opposite sex – causes tremendous frustration.

Harmonious functioning of the throat chakra

When the throat chakra is open and balanced, the person can express his emotions, his thoughts, his opinions, and his inner knowledge clearly, fearlessly, and freely. When the chakra is balanced, the person feels sure of himself. Therefore, he is not afraid to expose his weaknesses or his inner power to other people. Self-confidence, a good self-image, inner integrity, and integrity toward others characterize an open and balanced throat chakra.

When the chakra is open, the person can control his speech. He can remain silent and listen attentively to what other people are saying, and he does not feel the need to raise his voice in order to make himself heard. The self-expression that stems from the opening of the chakra is manifested in all areas of life. The person feels able to express his personality, his opinions, his faith, and his creativity, in every field – in his studies, in society, at work, and with his family. He feels a certain stability, and no manipulations can cause him to deviate from his opinions, beliefs, and the paths in which he believes. On the other hand, he feels sufficiently stable to listen to and accept different opinions (that are acceptable to him); he is not afraid that this will harm his individuality in any way, nor does he feel a need to stand up for himself stubbornly without a logical reason. He can communicate in a clear manner in order to attain his goals. His manner of speaking is creative, and he has a well-developed imagination, but, having said that, he knows how to suit his words to his listener. The things he says are clear and bright. His inner integrity serves him well, even when he encounters various difficulties or temptations that are liable to make him deviate from his path. He is able to set limits, say "no" when necessary – but he can also be flexible in his opinions and look for ways to bridge and compromise between different opinions.

When the throat chakra is open, the person feels free, self-standing, and independent of others. He is decisive and self-aware, and can acknowledge both his weaknesses and his talents and qualities. Freedom from prejudice, and the ability to shape his personal opinions with a free hand are also properties of an open throat chakra. There is a unity between emotion, reason, and thought, and the person is able to operate according to his reason and thought without feeling torn between them and his emotions – both sides are equal.

On the higher level, the throat chakra creates the ability to recognize the power of thought, the ability to control thought, and also to subdue it easily when it is necessary to enter states that require a lack thought (such as meditation). The link with the superego becomes clearer, and there is an ability to recognize the various messages that are sent by the universe. The person can use symbols and understand them, create and feel inspiration and the power of imagination, and even channel with entities or thought energies on various extraterrestrial planes. The ability to listen, which characterizes the open throat chakra, attains a new dimension on the highest level. The person can listen "between the lines," be totally attentive to the people speaking to him, and discover in their utterances content that is beyond mere words. He can discern the qualities of the voice and the sounds that accompany the word, and give it a deeper significance. This ability is essential for therapists, because the patient often indicates the source of his problem "incidentally" or drops a hint during the conversation. Conversely, it is possible to understand a great deal about his problems and their causes from the way he speaks.

An open throat chakra allows the person to feel the joy of expression in all its forms. He is not afraid of saying what he has to say from the standpoint of his inner truth; he is not afraid that his opinions will not be accepted, or will be rejected by others, and is able to transmit, explain, and illustrate his opinions, conclusions, and beliefs to other people.

An open throat chakra stimulates deep confidence and faith in the person. Since it is the first of the upper chakras, it links us to cosmic knowledge and to the understanding that things are far from being what they seem on the surface, in their material and physical form. The self-expressive ability creates a feeling of freedom and the ability to understand the different functions of the people in the world, and to be tolerant of their opinions and their feelings. It creates inner depth, profound understanding of the ways of the world, and a feeling of fullness, satisfaction, and confidence in the universe and its ways.

Unharmonious functioning of the throat chakra

When the throat chakra is in a state of disharmony, the person finds it difficult to express himself, his personality, and his uniqueness on the different levels. He is fraught with various communication problems, and two of them are liable to cause severe conflicts and even a serious lack of harmony in all areas of his life:

The first is the communication problem between the person and his body, communication that can be blocked or unharmonious. The person has difficulty listening to his body and to its natural needs and desires. This state can wear him down, and he may be unaware of the nature of his personal functioning – this can easily cause him to succumb to various diseases.

The second communication problem is the inability to create harmony and unity between emotion on the one hand, and thought and logic on the other. This state can cause the person to be unable to express his emotions, or his emotions to be illogical or unacceptable to him, making him prefer to lock himself into a world of pure logic and intellect in which there is no room for emotion. This state can also occur when the person expresses unsolved emotions in his thoughts, but is unable to express them physically and verbally. He is liable to daydream and hold imaginary conversations with the people to whom he wants to express his emotions, but is unable to actually express them to the object of his feelings.

The imbalance in the throat chakra can also be expressed in low self-esteem, in a negative self-image, and in perpetual self-criticism. The person feels that it is necessary to behave, act, and speak in a way that "suits" others in order to be accepted by them. He is afraid of expressing his true opinions, which may generate criticism that will damage his already shaky self-esteem. Sometimes, an imbalance in the chakra may be accompanied by guilt feelings or a fear of self-expression and of expressing his personality. This can lead him to "cover up" his true opinions and desires with overtalkativeness in order to hide his true meaning, about which he feels groundless guilt.

The disturbances in communication that are caused by an unbalanced throat chakra can also be expressed in language and speech. The person is liable to speak haltingly, feel that he is not succeeding in expressing his thoughts in a clear and comprehensible verbal manner. Sometimes, the imbalance can be expressed in precise, to-the-point speech, which camouflages the fear of using too many words in case any of them should be "incongruous." People whose throat chakras are unbalanced are likely to always speak very loudly, or to stutter under certain circumstances.

The need that occurs, when the chakra is not balanced, not to "betray" the person's weak points, weaknesses, and helplessness is liable to cause him to always appear to be strong. He is unable to let himself be supported by others when necessary. This can exert a great deal of pressure on him.

An imbalance in the throat chakra can also be characterized in overtalkativeness, and talking for the sake of attracting attention. Gossip, too, which results from a fear of "awkward silences," and the constant search for a topic of conversation, can occur. The person may display problems in listening, or may hear only what he wants to hear, or understand what people are saying in a superficial way only.

When the throat chakra is blocked or unbalanced in the extreme, there is little likelihood that the person will become aware of and acquainted with the more subtle layers of the universe. A blocked throat chakra leads to a lack of self-awareness, which does not permit a broad awareness of the universe. This does not mean that the person lacks knowledge or understanding, but he is afraid of expressing this knowledge, or has difficulty doing so. It is likely that his awareness is expressed mainly in the thought and philosophical layer, but not in his life.

Because of the difficulty in expressing emotions when the chakra is not balanced, the person may become bitter or suffer from emotional outbursts when the repressed emotions refuse to be ignored any longer. Conversely, the imbalance in the chakra may lead to apathy and indifference as a result of the lack of good communicative abilities that help the person understand other people and feel an affinity for them.

The colors of the chakra

The colors of the throat chakra are blue, light blue and turquoise. All the shades of blue, from the lightest to the darkest, are suitable for opening and balancing the throat chakra. For healing and projecting color, the deep blue of lapis lazuli is the most highly recommended, but the shade of blue must be matched to the patient. Of course, if a certain shade comes up intuitively during the treatment, it is almost certainly the shade that suits the patient personally.

Silver also helps reinforce the throat chakra, and it is especially suitable for treating throat infections and states of imbalance in the thyroid and parathyroid glands.

Blue is the color with the highest energy of all the colors of the spectrum, but its effect on the entire organism is the most soothing. Blue creates a feeling of calmness and expansiveness. It symbolizes depth and inward withdrawal, coolness, true, devotion, wisdom, rest, renewal, purity, inspiration, calmness and sleep. In higher layers of the throat chakra, it represents intuition, meditative ability, spiritual development, morality, honesty and spirituality. It assists in the treatment of a broad range of emotional and mental problems on the one hand and physical problems on the other.

Blue is widely used in color therapy for treating various mental states. It helps in attaining calmness and a feeling of tranquillity, in releasing tension, in treating insomnia, in developing abilities for communication with oneself and with others, and in awakening spiritual understanding and belief. Moreover, it is very suitable for treating hot-tempered people and people who find it difficult to calm down. When a person tends to suffer from the cold (or from cold in his extremities), projecting blue alone is liable to make the feeling of coldness more extreme both during and after the treatment. In addition, in certain situations, projecting blue alone may cause certain people to feel tired, slightly sluggish, or low. For this reason, every case must be examined on its own merits, and, if necessary, the complementary color – red – should projected with blue.

Blue helps lower blood pressure and slow down the heartbeat rate. It has a beneficial effect on the nervous system and can be used to solve problems connected with defective nerve functioning and even organic nervous problems. It is linked to the nerve cells, the brain, the spinal cord, the skin, the hair, and the sensory organs. It helps treat various throat problems, respiratory problems, and is used for treating hoarseness and vocal cord problems, hemorrhaging and pulmonary hemorrhages (not as a substitute for medical care, of course), for lowering fever and treating inflammations, for treating bruises, burns and sunburn, for cases of swelling accompanied by pain, for constipation and diarrhea, for treating hepatitis, for strengthening and shrinking tissues, for slowing down the development of tumors, and for treating sensory and emotional disturbances. It is one of the most important colors for treating a range of female problems and diseases, and is very helpful in treating menstrual pains and menopausal problems. It helps greatly with relaxation, and can be used in color projection when the person is tense and finds it difficult to calm down during treatment. Moreover, it is cooling in cases of heat and feverishness.

When the throat chakra is open and balanced, the blue color may appear brightly and strongly around the chakra, and may be evident in the higher parts of the aura. In such cases, blue attests to inner balance, calmness, tranquillity, confidence, patience, trust, honesty, reliability, and an aspiration for truth. It may also attest to love, wisdom, courtesy, an ability to concentrate intensely, cooperation, sensitivity, forgiveness, devotion, an ability to see and assess what is going on correctly, inner quietness and inner repose, and highly developed faith and spiritual awareness. When the throat chakra is not balanced, and the color blue appears either unbalanced and overly dominant in the aura or faded, dull, and covered with dark clouds, it may attest to a person who suffers from fears and anxiety, self-pity, loneliness and isolation, depression, a tendency toward melancholy, a lack of self-confidence, a lack of involvement, a lack of interest in what is going on, exaggerated restraint, an inability to express emotions, emotional frigidity and passivity.

The shades of light blue are also used for treating the throat chakra. It contains all the properties of the color blue, and, in addition, helps lower blood pressure significantly (mainly sky blue). Sky blue, with its delicate frequencies, opens the mind, induces a feeling of freedom and calmness, and is wonderful for calming and reducing pressure. When light blue that tends toward sky blue appears around the chakra and among the colors of the aura, it symbolizes qualities that are similar to the qualities of blue, but also attests to softness, developed spirituality, sometimes a powerful attraction to religion, powerful faith, idealism and devotion to ideas and beliefs. When it appears around the chakra in a less balanced way, it may attest to a certain tendency to float. It sometimes attests to bashfulness, conservativeness, isolation and a need to get away from the crowd.

Turquoise, too, is a wonderful color for balancing and opening the throat chakra. It often appears intuitively during color projection, especially in cases in which the patient needs some kind of protection, or when he is found to have healing powers that need to be stimulated. Moreover, since turquoise contains blue – the color of the throat chakra, and green – the color of the heart chakra, it may be used in treatment with color projection for balancing and stimulating both chakras together and for creating a link between the chakras and releasing the blockages between them, which may be expressed in the creation of a separation between emotion and reason.

Turquoise is a soothing color that affords a feeling of protection, cools body and mind, helps lower fever and treat cases of fever, soothes anger and irritation, helps treat headaches, restores beauty, rehabilitates the skin, treats swellings, bites and stings, soothes attacks of irritation and treats burns and sunstroke. When it appears around the chakra and among the colors of the aura in a harmonious and balanced way, it may attest to a wonderful combination of the qualities of the heart chakra and the throat chakra, to healing and curing abilities, to creative communication, to a great deal of caring for other people, to the use of the power of expression for the sake of other people, to great creativity, to a profound understanding of the laws of the universe as a result of observing nature and its laws, to innovation and the ability for renewal and constant growth, to a great love of esthetics, to a *joie de vivre* that stems from faith and security, to creative cooperation, to calmness that is combined with action, to assertiveness and to the love of humankind.

The connection between the throat chakra and the physical body

The throat chakra is linked to the following organs and influences them: the throat, the neck, the vocal cords and vocal organs, the thyroid gland, the parathyroid glands, the jaw, the upper part of the lungs, the nerves, the ears, the muscles, and the arms. An imbalance in the throat chakra is expressed in a tendency toward numerous throat inflammations, infections and problems in the vocal organs, an imbalance in the thyroid gland (hypothyroidism or hyperthyroidism), lung problems, auditory problems, ear infections and problems, speech impediments and problems, stuttering, lung infections, tense muscles, neck pains, tension in the neck muscles, problems in the arms, and various nervous problems.

Fears of expression tend to become "trapped" in the throat muscles. This creates a blockage of emotions and thoughts, disrupts the natural energy flow, and creates limitations in natural expression. The throat is the organ through which we make our voice heard and express our thoughts, emotions, and desires. We express our creativity, our individuality, our personal opinions and our world-view through our throat. When there is a serious conflict between emotion and reason, or when there is repressed anger – a desire to express something, and a blockage of the desire – the expressive ability is harmed, and this can be manifested in throat problems. The throat is the center for our ability to change. It is located between the head and the heart, and for this reason must express flexibility and an ability to clarify our opinions and the way in which they fit into our personal lives. Rigidity and obstinacy, an unwillingness to change – even when the heart and mind indicate the need to do so – can also be at the root of various throat and neck problems. This is also the case when the person feels that he is unable to express his self and demand the fulfillment of his wishes. This is the function of the throat – to enable us to express what is in our heart, to speak for ourselves, and to present our opinions, desires, and thoughts. When a person stops himself from doing that, out of fear of his surroundings and of the way in which his demands or opinions will be received, he sabotages the original and basic action of this organ. This state is likely to be one of the causes of throat infections, especially recurrent ones. In such cases, it should be checked whether or not the person feels and understands his natural (and essential) right to speak for himself and express his desires, emotions, and opinions freely. Often, this is the source of chronic throat infections in children whose parents tend to speak for them, decide for them, or hush them up through criticism (in a direct verbal manner, or indirectly) when the child expresses his wishes or thoughts.

Losing one's voice is another problem that is linked to the action of the throat chakra. Like various throat problems, it may stem from continuously suppressed extreme rage and anger, to the point that vocal expression is prevented for fear that if the voice is released, the suppressed feelings of rage will also be. This condition sometimes stems from a deep, basic fear of making oneself heard, or from a trauma that caused this fear. Unfocussed thinking and an inability to concentrate can cause a person to lose his voice, because of a lack of knowledge of the direction in which he wishes to direct his voice in order for it to hit a particular target and express a certain wish.

Similar to the throat, the neck also symbolizes flexibility because of the fact that it enables us to look forward, backward, and sideways. When a person suffers from severe neck problems, tension, stiffness, and recurrent cramps that are not a result of prolonged physical over-exertion of the throat, it is necessary to check and see whether there are things "behind" him that he cannot look at, or if exaggerated obstinacy is inhibiting his development.

The emotional layer that represents jaw problems can also stem from an extreme repression of self-expression. The person feels that he has a lot to say – an emotional bottleneck and a large emotional burden that stems from unresolved conflicts between him and the figures who play a significant role in his life – but he grits his teeth and, with great difficulty, bottles up the emotional storm that threatens to erupt. Thought patterns that are full of vengeance, resentment, and rage can also cause various jaw problems, and are sometimes manifested in jaw-clenching during sleep.

Halitosis, when there is no obvious physiological reason for it (such as tooth decay or digestive problems) may well be connected to the functioning of the throat chakra in conjunction with an imbalance in the functioning of the heart chakra. This state may be an expression of unclean thoughts, venomous attitudes, and the habitual and frequent use of the mouth to expel mental "garbage" such as malicious gossip or hurtful, venomous words.

Problems in the mouth may also be connected to the state of the throat chakra. The mouth represents the way in which we receive nutrition – physically, emotionally, and spiritually – and the ability to absorb new ideas. Problems that are connected to the mouth may be the embodiment of narrow-mindedness, a lack of openness to new ideas, and stagnation of thought.

Stuttering is also a problem that can occur in cases of a significant imbalance in the throat chakra – occasionally in conjunction with a significant imbalance in the heart, sexual, or solar plexus chakras, or all of them. Stuttering may represent a deep lack of confidence generally, fear of expressing personal opinions, or the inability to express profound emotions. In the latter case, stuttering can occur when the person is trying to express his feelings about a particular person or matter.

The thyroid gland is the gland that is linked to the throat chakra. The hormones it produces are essential for maintaining the correct rate of metabolism in the body and for determining the body's rate of activity. Moreover, the hormones it produces increase the consumption of oxygen and the production of protein. Thyroid problems are often linked to a feeling of humiliation – the feeling of being "last in line" to fulfill wishes and desires, a constant need to take the desires and needs of others into account because of a low self-image and a feeling of worthlessness that causes the person to attract situations that "compel" him to forego his needs.

Hypothyroidism is a condition in which the thyroid gland is underactive, and metabolism – the symbol of our ability to receive and give in a balanced way in our life – becomes extremely slow (this occurs mainly in women). This condition represents resigning oneself to a lack of self-expression, not standing up for one's personal opinions, and not fulfilling one's natural desires and demands.

Hyperthyroidism, a condition in which the gland is overactive and causes an acceleration of metabolism, expresses a kind of "war" and inner resistance to this situation – resistance to the feeling of humiliation or oppression – a war that is waged without solving the basic reasons for being in the given situation. The person feels that he has to fight because of a feeling of no inner hope, in order to be "first in line," starting with his basic family unit and ending with his job, and in order to fulfill his desires here and now, as well as his capacity for self-expression.

Goiter, another thyroid disease, represents an extreme feeling of humiliation or the person's personal wishes being ignored by those around him – a feeling of exploitation. The person feels that he has to satisfy everyone else's wishes and do things for them, while no one wants to take his wishes into consideration and "do things for him." Of course, this situation expresses an unconscious perception of the laws of the exchange of energy between people – a state of constant weighing up "what he did for me, and what I did for him," which also causes a problem of unbalanced metabolism in the body. In the case of goiter, the feeling of oppression and exploitation is liable to turn almost into a physical mass of hatred toward the "exploiter" or the "oppressor." Moreover, goiter – which stems from the thyroid gland not receiving sufficient iodine, which it needs for its existence, and therefore creates a goiter whose job it is to absorb more and more iodine – can express a feeling of dissatisfaction with life. What there is in one's present life is not enough for a full and balanced existence. As we said before, the disease may manifest itself as a pattern of "rebellion" against the suppression of self-expression.

Deafness and auditory problems are also linked to an imbalance in the throat chakra. Deafness symbolizes a rejection of the desire to hear, and a desire to withdraw and close oneself off from the world. It is possible that, in the person's past, there were too many "painful" auditory stimuli, such as serious rows between his parents, family "secrets" that it was forbidden to reveal, verbal abuse, severe verbal humiliation, and so on. These things cause the feeling of "it would have been better if I hadn't heard." This may be manifested in different levels of hearing impairment, in accordance with the oppression and the messages or contents that were difficult to process emotionally, as well as with the person's level of sensitivity (or the child, as he was when these traumatic events occurred). Sometimes, auditory problems express a feeling of excessive tiresome external stimuli, incessant parental verbiage that prevented the child from concentrating on himself, and "do's" and "don'ts" regarding everything, especially with children. Sometimes this is the reason for recurrent ear infections in small children, who are actually asking for a bit of peace and quiet.

The arms are also linked to the throat chakra. They represent our ability to hold onto various life experiences in order to learn a mental lesson from them (instead of perceiving this holding on as inhibiting or traumatic). A blocked and unaware mental ability to interpret life's experiences, feeling that life's difficult experiences are a burden, and a desire to throw in the towel and let things pass us by instead of grabbing hold of them and delving into them, can manifest themselves in various problems in the arms.

Many respiratory problems are linked to the action of the throat chakra in conjunction with a state of imbalance in the heart chakra. Breathing represents our ability to experience life fully.

Muscle stiffness may often be connected to rigid and inflexible thinking. Muscle degeneration is also linked, in certain layers, to the action of the throat chakra. It may derive from a loss of belief and faith in life, from a profound lack of confidence, from pessimistic, gloomy, and inhibiting thoughts that quench all desire to take an additional step in life, and from resistance to the joy of life that creates mobility. This state is also likely to stem from a tremendous need for "control," and also involves a profound imbalance in the solar plexus chakra.

The nerves, some of whose functions are linked to the action of the throat chakra, represent communication and the willingness to absorb. Nerve pains may derive from emotional pain whose source lies in deficient communication, or from guilt or punitive feelings that lead to an imbalance in the ability to communicate – emission and reception. The emotional parallel of a nervous breakdown may be the blockage of the communication channels, the breakdown of the desire to communicate with the outside world, or exaggerated preoccupation with the self.

In addition, there is a connection between sexual problems and the functioning of the throat chakra. Often, an imbalance in the sexual chakra parallels an imbalance in the throat chakra. Both chakras activate expression and creation, in different and complementary layers, so during treatment of sexual problems and problems concerning masculinity and femininity, the sexual chakra must be examined as well as the interaction between the two chakras. As we stated previously, the throat chakra is very important in our self-image, and some of the feminine or masculine sexual problems are linked to this layer of the person's soul.

The influence of the chakra on hormonal activity

The hormonal glands linked to the throat chakra are the thyroid and parathyroid glands.

The thyroid gland is located in the anterior part of the neck, and consists of two joined lobes. It is formed from the tongue in the fetus – part of the tongue becomes the thyroid gland. It is formed in the hollow of the mouth and moves downward until it locates itself in the neck. The gland contains follicles in which there is a substance that contains a large supply of the thyroid hormones triiodo-thyronine (T3) and thyroxine (T4). The thyroid is the only gland in the body that contains a large supply of these hormones. The amount stored in the gland is sufficient for the body's needs for three months. In order to produce the hormones, the gland requires two substances: Thyroid-stimulating hormone (TSH) or thyrotropin – a hormone that is secreted by the pituitary – and iodine – which the body absorbs from food, and is absorbed only by the thyroid gland because only this gland needs it. Inside the thyroid gland, the iodine synthesizes the two hormones, T3 and T4. The hormones are very important for the development of the brain and bones in babies. A lack of thyroid hormone in a newborn causes mental retardation and distortions in the development of the skeleton. In the adult, the hormone determines the body's "rate of action." On the cellular level, the hormone increases oxygen consumption and protein production. The role of these hormones in maintaining the correct rate of metabolism is absolutely vital.

The production of the hormone is regulated by the hypothalamus in the brain, which secretes a stimulating hormone called thyrotropin-releasing hormone (TRH). The latter causes the pituitary gland to secrete TSH, which causes the thyroid gland to secrete the thyroid hormones. A decrease in the amount of thyroid hormones in the blood causes a rise in the secretion of stimulating hormones, and vice versa.

The parathyroid glands are located on the thyroid itself, and dispatch the hormone that is responsible for the calcium level in the blood. The calcium levels in the blood plasma affect the activity of all the muscles in the body, including the heart muscle.

Thyroxine, a thyroid hormone, affects all aspects of the metabolism in the body, body temperature, and various growth factors. When the level of the hormone in the body is too high, as in cases of hyperthyroidism, the body has a tendency toward stress and over-activity that is likely to express itself in agitation, hair loss, increased appetite with weight loss, diarrhea, tremors in the hands, almost perpetual perspiration, an intolerance of heat, a fast heart rate, and exophthalmia (protruding eyes).

Too little of the hormone thyroxine causes all the body's activities including metabolism to be slower. In this situation, which is called hypothyroidism, there is a heavy feeling of fatigue, a lack of appetite with weight gain, hair loss, balding, swelling, slower speech, thickening of the voice, constipation, irregular menstrual cycle, sensitivity to cold, and major susceptibility to viral infections. (Note that every viral disease constitutes a mortal threat to the patient, because his immune system does not function properly.) This disease is more common among women.

Another disease of the thyroid gland is goiter. This disease occurs mainly when there is insufficient iodine in the food, or the ability to absorb iodine is impaired, and the thyroid gland grows in order to store more and more iodine.

Meditations

Linking up to the throat chakra

In order to be familiar with the state of the throat chakra, it is important to become profoundly "acquainted" with it. To this end, free up about 10 minutes during which you will not be disturbed. Perform the meditation in a quiet, well-ventilated room. It is a good idea to use one of the aromatic oils that soothes or stimulates the action of the chakra.

Sit or lie down comfortably and relax your body. Take deep, slow breaths, feeling the air flowing through your throat chakra. Imagine the chakra to be a beautiful lotus flower in a shade of blue, with 16 petals. See the petals of the chakra turning toward the front, to the anterior part of the throat, and the stem turning toward the nape of the neck, descending, and joining up with the central column. Observe the blue color of the chakra. What shade of blue appears in the chakra? Dark blue, sky blue, turquoise, or some other shade of blue? What does this shade of blue evoke in you? Do you feel at one and comfortable with it? Pay attention to the "cleanness" of the color – is it faded or stained with dark or cloudy spots? Commit the shade of the chakra to memory and, if you do not feel comfortable with the shade or with the faded or unclear color, begin to work toward changing it, using your imagination. If the color of the chakra is weak, begin to make blue light flow into it. With each inhalation, see blue light penetrating your head from above, and surrounding the chakra, filling it and merging with it. If you noticed dark spots in the color of the chakra, exhale them. Continue doing this for as long as necessary.

Now look at the chakra's petals. Are they all wide open or partially closed? Try to open them. You can open them during inhalation – with each inhalation, see the petals gradually opening. Another way is to inhale a large amount of air, and exhale it while intoning the sound "Eh...", noticing how the sound causes the petals of the chakra to vibrate, stimulating them to open. Keep on doing this until all the petals are open, or until you feel a sincere desire to stop. As we said, the process of opening, cleaning and stimulating the chakra may not be completed in only one meditation. This is natural and commonplace. Even if progress was slow, you can feel the change in your everyday life, in your abilities and powers of expression, and in your self-image.

Conclude the meditation with several deep breaths, feeling that each breath is cleaning and purifying your throat chakra. Continue sitting or lying down for a few minutes until you feel ready to get up.

During the course of the meditation, various contents may arise: memories, thoughts, ideas. Do not focus on them, but remember them so that you can write them down after you have completed the meditation.

In order to complete the process, it is a good idea to activate the chakra a bit immediately after the meditation, for a length of time that seems appropriate and convenient. Do this by singing, humming, laughing, shouting, imitating sounds, speaking, or even crying. You can recite a poem you love, and sing the words along with the music. Reading a chapter from a book or even a newspaper article will help to continue stimulating the chakra and causing its petals to open further. While you are activating your chakra in these ways, it is very important to concentrate on your voice and to be aware of how you breathe when you make vocal sounds. (Do you "allow" yourself to breathe? Do you provide yourself with the necessary amount of air for these activities?) Be aware of the sensations that arise in you. If the chakra tends to be blocked or partially closed, a feeling of unease and even of shame may occur while you are doing these exercises. If you notice this feeling, you should memorize one or more of the following mantras: "I make my voice heard easily and lovingly." "I own my voice, I express my voice happily." "I love and admire myself, I express my creativity naturally and lovingly." Those are just general examples of positive thoughts that help change negative patterns that have accumulated in the throat chakra over the years, every time we refrained from making our voice heard and expressing ourselves. You can change the mantras as you please or invent similar ones that are tailor-made for you. Remember to say them in a positive way (that is, do not say, "I am *not afraid* of making my voice heard"), since our subconscious tends to ignore various auxiliaries and pick up the word that is uttered literally (in this example, the subconscious will pick up the word "afraid" instead of "not afraid").

If you discover that your throat chakra tends to be blocked or generally closed, you should repeat the meditation and the exercises every day for a week, or once every two days for ten days. Over time, you will feel and see beneficial progress.

The sixth chakra

The third eye chakra

Ajna

The third eye chakra ·····················

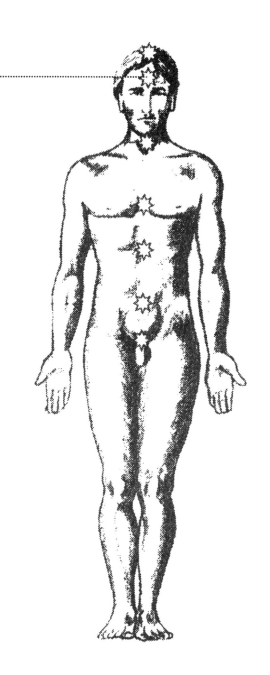

Location of the chakra: The center of the forehead.

Colors: Indigo, purple.

Symbol: A sky-blue circle surrounded on each side by two large lotus petals (or a lotus with 96 petals – each large lotus petal represents 48 petals), and inside it a picture of two feet. From the circle, the chakra's stem emerges.

Key words: Inspiration, spirituality, awareness, command, perfection.

Basic principles: Existential awareness.

Inner aspect: Extrasensory communication.

Energy: Intuition.

Element: Radium.

Sense: Intuition (the "sixth sense"), and all the senses in their most subtle significance.

Sound: "Ham-ksham."

Body: The high mental body.

Nerve plexus: The central nervous system.

Hormonal glands linked to the chakra: The pituitary gland and the pineal gland.

Body organs linked to the chakra: The brain and all its components, the central nervous system, the face, the eyes, the ears, the nose, the sinuses.

Problems and diseases that occur during an imbalance of the chakra: Eye diseases, ear diseases, respiratory tract problems, nose and sinus problems, facial nerve problems, headaches, nightmares.

Essential oils: Geranium, lavender, spearmint, rosemary.

Crystals and stones: Amethyst, azurite, fluorite, lapidolite, sugilite.

Stars and astrological signs linked to the chakra: The planets that are associated with the third eye chakra are Jupiter, Uranus, Mercury (because it symbolizes intellectual perception and logical thought), and Neptune, and the Zodiac signs are Sagittarius, Aquarius, and Pisces.

Sagittarius, which is dominated by the planet Jupiter, is linked to the chakra because of its comprehensive, holistic thinking ability, as well as its ability to understand inner processes.

Aquarius, which is dominated by the planet Uranus, is linked to the chakra because it symbolizes thinking that is full of inspiration from superior sources, superior knowledge, and developed intuition.

Pisces, which is dominated by the planet Neptune, symbolizes the chakra because of its developed intuition, richness of imagination, and the devotion that leads to higher truths.

The third eye chakra is located on the point between the eyes, slightly above the line of the eyes. Its stem descends along the length of the back of the head. The meaning of its name in Sanskrit, Ajna, is "command center."

The sixth chakra is responsible for conscious perception. It oversees the various mental abilities, memory, willpower, and knowledge. This is the chakra that connects the person to his subconscious, to his intuition, to the ability to understand cosmic insights, and receive non-verbal messages. It is responsible for the balance between the two cerebral hemispheres, the right and the left, that is, between intuition, emotion, and mysticism on the one hand, and reason and logic on the other. It is responsible for the person's physical balance, ability to concentrate, peace of mind, and wisdom.

The third eye chakra induces a desire for a feeling of wholeness, which stems from the perfect harmony of the universe. When the third eye chakra is blocked, people cannot imagine that this is possible. They live their lives by constantly struggling, compromising, resigning themselves – and see the existing reality as the only reality, which is obvious and cannot be changed by any force other than physical force and the force of practical action. When the chakra is opened, the person finds that he wants to feel in harmony with the universe, and first and foremost with himself.

The opening of the chakra arouses many questions. The desire for perfection is first expressed as a desire for self-perfection, self-integrity, and for faith in what the person does and in the feeling that he does not live for himself alone; there are higher powers at work in the universe. Man is part of these forces because of his soul. The awakening of the soul – or, more precisely, the awakening of the awareness of the soul – causes the person to query his vocation in life, and he often feels that so-called "ordinary" life – accumulating assets, financial security, work, status, and so on – is not enough. Sometimes this awakening creates a certain crisis, similar to the crisis that the person is likely to experience when his throat chakra is opened and balanced, when he realizes that in fact he does not express himself and his personality entirely. But this crisis is one of "recovery" – it leads to new insights, to openness that permits a deeper scrutiny of everything that is going on, and significant development of the awareness in all the layers. The quest for harmony that occurs when the third eye chakra is opened and balanced signifies a desire for the holistic harmony of body, mind, emotion, soul, and spirit.

The third eye chakra has a higher role in everything concerning creation – it is the one that links us to inspiration. The opening of the base chakra enables us to see to our basic and material needs in the physical layers of the universe, and to create our material world, which grants security and vitality. The opening of the sexual chakra enables us to express our creative powers as a result of self-discovery, adventurousness, curiosity, and understanding change. The opening of the solar plexus chakra enables us to recognize our inner strength and our personal power, and inspires in us the desire to create, while the heart and throat chakras require personal expression, and channels this personal expression into an array of artistic paths. Those same artistic paths into which the person wants to channel his physical, emotional, and spiritual energies all exist in the universe, in different forms. Movement, color, sound, structure, and all their derivatives, constitute part of the physical world, as well as the energetic and spiritual world.

The third eye chakra stimulates inspiration. As a result of inspiration, creation from nothing is possible – the creation of new worlds, inventiveness, the expression of higher insights and presenting them in forms that are somewhat comprehensible to other people, and the ability to receive messages from other worlds and other times – future or past – from distant places that the artist's eye did not see physically. The more open and balanced the third eye chakra is, the easier it is to enter a state of inspiration, which is known to many creators as a state that is timeless – like a meditative state in which an abundance of ideas take shape by themselves.

As we mentioned previously, the meaning of the Sanskrit name for the third eye chakra is "command center." On the physical level, this chakra is the command center for the action of the central nervous system. It oversees the regular activity of this system, which activates all of our perceptive and cerebral activities, and, of course, the senses. In addition, the opening and balancing of this chakra enables us to "take command" of our lives, possible only after we have understood the laws of the universe. As a result of the chakra being open, we can clearly see how we create our reality, and how we physically live the perception of our so-called "cerebral" world. Many people feel that they are in control of their lives, but in many cases, the opposite is true. The true "commanders" are the emotions or the thoughts that came into being during that life as a result of various life experiences and circumstances. When the chakra is open, the person can discern when his emotions – or non-supportive thoughts, as well as social norms, various acquired patterns, and so on – are in control. As a result of this ability to discern, he can sift out what is not "his" in the full meaning of the word – what does not belong to his soul fully and unequivocally. Equally, he can begin to discover what is "his": his true vocation, his true belief, the laws of the universe according to which the world operates (as does our life in its wake whether we like it or not). This ability to comprehend is tremendous, since it enables the person not only to realize his life according to his personal will, but also to realize it according to the will of the universe, which becomes his will.

As we stated before, the third eye chakra has supreme responsibility for the activity of our physical senses. On the spiritual level, this chakra is responsible for our intuitive ability, our extrasensory perceptive ability, and our ability to use our extrasensory senses. Just as the physical body has energetic parallels, so the physical senses have parallel, more subtle senses.

All knowledge exists in the universe. The ability to receive knowledge depends on the person's capacity, and on his ability to connect to those sources of knowledge via the third eye.

The vast knowledge that exists in the universe – in sight, sound, and sensation – is realized in sound, touch, and smell. We experience those senses through our physical senses. However, each one of these senses exists in a more subtle form, in which the limits of time and space do not exist. The higher spiritual function of the third eye chakra is its ability to link up to these senses and activate them, and as a result receive vast, important knowledge, without being dependent on where we are, when we are living, or the physical condition of our physical senses.

The extrasensory visual ability (clairvoyance) is expressed in numerous ways. It can appear in dreams and meditations, and enables us to see things that are happening in other places, as well as at other times, including past lives or the future. Sometimes, this ability is activated when someone close to us needs us or is in danger. When the ability is more developed, the person can use it when he is awake as well by entering a meditative state, or with flashes of vision. Additional layers of this ability contain the ability to see various entities and auras, and look into the interior of objects or bodies.

The extrasensory auditory ability (clairaudience) permits us to pick up selected frequencies from among the infinity of sound frequencies that exist in the universe. It may be expressed in the ability to hear those who are near and dear to us, to whom we are connected with a direct, strong, and consciously based energetic link – or even the ability to hear divine sounds and messages from other worlds or from spiritual entities. When the physical auditory sense becomes increasingly refined, it leads to more "holistic" hearing – that is, hearing and absorbing more of the words that are spoken, and understanding the meaning of the frequencies of the speaker's voice. Occasionally, this understanding is so acute that the listener is able to diagnose physical, emotional, and spiritual conditions according to the speaker's voice only. In addition, the clairaudient can pick up and hear what is not said physically, but rather only in thought, because what is said in thought is actually the energy of speech before it takes a concrete form.

Our ability to feel, the tactile sense, is a sense that can be highly developed. In its subtle layer, when the third eye chakra is performing its spiritual function, it permits the person to feel the different energies. This ability is used by many touch therapists. When we touch the recipient's body, we can discover the location of the physical blockages, muscle tension, warm and cold areas and so on through the tactile sense. When the tactile sense becomes increasingly refined, it enables us to touch the energy that flows from the various organs. Using this ability, it is possible to feel the subtle bodies and sense their condition, as well as the auric field of people and objects.

The sense of smell enables us to pick up different smells that occur as signs and symbols. The smell that is associated with the limbic system in the brain, the seat of the emotions, goes far beyond the action of smelling. We can smell something and suddenly feel overwhelmed by memories or emotions. This is because the sense of smell stimulates the limbic system, and "pulls" experiences that are associated with a certain smell out of it. In its subtle spiritual meaning, it enables us to smell things that do not exist physically. These smells sometimes occur as messages or symbols from worlds beyond.

The more open and balanced our third eye chakra is, the more openly and broadly our feelings can pick up events that do not occur in front of our physical eyes. The ability to pick up telepathic messages, in its different layers, is one of the expressions of the action of the third eye chakra. Telepathy enables us to "link up" to a certain frequency, to absorb it, and to process it consciously. The greater the awareness of the frequency, the clearer the nature of that sometimes vague "feeling" the person feels when another entity (human or other) tries to make contact with him. As the ability develops, it becomes possible to transmit an "answer" to the message that was picked up.

The ability to experience is not one of the senses, but rather includes all of the physical senses by adding the personal interpretative ability to what is happening. In the spiritual layer of this ability, it enables us to experience, consciously and through non-communication and separation of consciousness, experiences that we did not undergo personally or physically. Through this ability, all the abilities of the spiritual senses link up to create a perfect picture of events. This can be illustrated by the dream state. In certain dreams, the person feels as if he is undergoing the experience that is occurring. He sees a certain sight, hears the voices (or thoughts) that are spoken, sometimes feels tactile sensations, and is somewhat emotionally involved in what is happening. The spiritual ability of the experience enables us to experience another person's situation by holding an object that belongs to him, by observing or speaking to him, or through meditative states. It enables us to re-experience events from other lives, events from before we were born, and events that happened to us in the past. The last type of experience is familiar to almost everyone. We can re-experience, sometimes almost as intensely as in the original experience, a certain experience from the past, just by recalling it.

Thus it is obvious that the extrasensory experiences that are familiar to us – such as telepathy, astral journeys, psychokinesis (the influence of the power of thought on physical matter), prophecy, and prediction of the future, and so on – are affected by the condition of the third eye chakra. Of course, the cleaner a channel for receiving and transmitting messages the person is, the more clearly these abilities can be realized in him. While it is true that some of these abilities are "gifts" that are given to people on different levels, everyone can develop his spiritual senses to a certain extent, together with the ability to develop spiritual gifts they have been given.

Harmonious functioning of the third eye chakra

A state of balance of the third eye chakra, even if it is not completely open, is expressed in a good intellectual, cerebral, and philosophical ability, in an ability for research or invention, in clarity of thought, in high morality, in having good social roots, and in the ability to easily establish ties with people. One of the most obvious characteristics of the balance of the chakra is the intuitive ability, in all its manifestations. A balanced and open chakra (even partially) gives the person:

a good imaginative and visualization ability;

an ability to understand that is not only cerebral, logical, and rational, but also intuitive;

the ability to understand the embodiment of matter in the universe as a physical embodiment of the spiritual world;

idealistic thought;

free and creative imagination;

flexible thought;

the ability to see things from different angles;

the ability to discern how our thoughts, perceptions, and imagination exist and are realized in reality, through understanding the power of thought and imagination.

As the third eye chakra becomes increasingly open, endless perceptive experiences become available to the person. Things are interpreted entirely differently from those familiar "rational" perceptions, as a result of the ability to see beyond, above, and below what is happening.

The various intuitive abilities, together with the opening of the subtle senses, increase, and the person is able, according to his will (and not against his will) to receive intuitive messages that permit him to channel on different levels of awareness. The physical world is perceived as one world among the tremendous number of existing worlds. The insight that there are many different forms of life becomes clearer and more natural, to the point that in different layers of awareness, the person is given the opportunity to make contact with these forms of life and entities. The ability to feel, see, channel, and direct energies becomes clearer and more natural. The person can see the physical embodiment of his acts, emotions, and thoughts clearly, and as a result of deep insight, can match these layers to the action of the universe and to his cosmic vocation.

The ability to understand and even see previous lives increases, and the person is open to receiving messages from the universe, from his superego, from his soul and from his spirit. This can happen while he is sleeping, in dreams and meditations, and even when he is awake, as a result of understanding these messages, and the ability to use them in a useful way to repair his soul in this world and realize his cosmic vocation. Life experiences are perceived as lessons, as visions, as "learning aids," and as such, do not arouse inhibiting feelings, but rather the joy of learning and the ability to learn cosmic lessons that leads to the continuation of spiritual development.

As we said previously, there is no end to the tremendous abilities that take shape in the person when the third eye chakra is opened. When it is balanced and open, life becomes a marvelous experience, without a dull moment.

Unharmonious functioning of the third eye chakra

When the third eye chakra is not balanced, the person is likely to experience his life via his intellect, rationality, and logic. He feels a need for order and logic in everything he does, and things that do not fulfill these criteria (such as some of the theories in this book) may seem absolutely impossible to him. He requires clear, logical proof of things. He has to see them with his own eyes or feel them with his own hands in order to digest, understand, and grasp them. In cases of a serious imbalance, emotion, too, and not just intuition, seems "illogical" to the person. Sometimes, this state can lead to an extremely limited, clear, and obvious perception of the world – everything that does not operate according to this perception simply does not make sense. Everything connected with spirituality is likely to be rejected out of hand as "not logical," or "unscientific." Despite the progress of science today, which provides step-by-step scientific proof of many of the spiritual theories, when the third eye chakra functions unharmoniously, even supplying scientific proof will not enable the person to understand these perceptions in depth.

Another condition of an unbalanced third eye chakra can – ironically – be manifested in the ability for basic understanding of spiritual truths, but only superficially. It may be accompanied by the desire to use powers of thought to influence events or people, to satisfy personal desires, to inspire awe or admiration, or to satisfy any other self-interest. This state generally goes hand in hand with an unbalanced solar plexus chakra, which causes the person to want to control and manipulate people and situations, and with the heart chakra, which is functioning in a serious state of lack or blockage. Among the people who suffer from this kind of imbalance in the third eye chakra are charlatans, who use their power to satisfy their selfish desires. The person whose third eye chakra is open properly never wants to use his intellectual or spiritual powers for any manipulation whatsoever. This is because a balanced state of the third eye chakra leads to a profound understanding of the laws of the universe, which do not tolerate this kind of manipulation under any circumstances. It also leads to a clear understanding of the danger, both personal and universal, that is inherent in the abuse of the power of thought or of the intuitive powers.

Sometimes, a situation may arise in which the third eye chakra is partially open, but is unbalanced, while the rest of the chakras, especially the lower ones, are not balanced. This can lead to a general imbalance, "floating," a lack of grounding, and an inability to understand the messages that are picked up by the intuition. A situation is also likely to arise in which the person cannot distinguish between genuine messages and visions that are the fruit of his imagination. He is liable to create various scenes in his imaginings, perceive them as genuine, and lose contact with reality.

A more widespread occurence is where the imbalance in the third eye chakra causes a lack of confidence in the universe and a lack of deep understanding of events. This lack of confidence may manifest itself in various anxieties, a lack of serenity, fear of the future, indecisiveness, agitation, constant tension, and cynicism.

The colors of the chakra

The color of the third eye chakra is indigo, but the color purple also appears in the chakra occasionally and can be used for balancing and stimulating it. Indigo appears in the color spectrum (but it difficult to distinguish from the rest of the colors), and its shade is a kind of deep blue with a tendency toward purple. The color is produced from the indigo plant, after which it is named. Indigo stimulates the flow of the mind's energy through the sixth chakra and affects the ability to see and experience visions, as well as the senses of hearing and smell on the physical, astral and spiritual planes. It symbolizes healing abilities, unity, inspiration, rest, balance, synthesis, inner tranquillity and inner peace, seriousness, kindness, morality, and purity of intentions. It affects the senses of hearing, sight and smell. Its range of therapeutic uses for various physical problems extends over all the problems that derive from an imbalance or blockage in the third eye chakra – ear, nose, and eye problems, problems with the nervous system and problems connected to hearing, sight, and smell. It helps treat problems of fever that stem from the lymph glands, is very effective for purifying the circulatory system and for regulating metabolism and cell replacement in the body, and helps treat disturbances in the respiratory system. In color projection, it can be used for freeing the person of negative burdens of color that he accumulated in the past and balancing all the colors.

When indigo appears in the region of the third eye chakra and among the colors of the aura in a harmonious and balanced manner, it indicates a person who enjoys inner tranquillity and inner peace, a feeling of unity and inspiration, emotional and spiritual balance, caring, morality and a feeling of vocation. It attest to a person who wants to be an active part of the universe and operate according to its laws, who aspires to help humanity, who has powerful intuition and healing abilities, and sometimes has an ability to see auras and visions and pick up divine messages. Indigo can also appear around the chakra in an unbalanced way, when it is faded or misty or stained with dark spots. These states may indicate that the person suffers from a domineering attitude, pride, arrogance, exaggerated restraint, tyranny, and sometimes makes selfish and improper use of intuitive powers.

Sometimes yellow may appear around the third eye chakra. It attests to a certain level of awareness, generally intellectual and rational thinking. When deep blue appears in the region of the chakra, it may attest to a holistic perception, powerful intuition and empathy for other people that is expressed in the desire to help others in mental and spiritual processes.

Purple (in its pure form, not indigo) is also one of the colors of the third eye chakra, and may appear in the region of the chakra. Purple is also one of the colors of the crown chakra, and for this reason may attest to especially developed spirituality when it appears in the region of the third eye chakra. Occasionally it appears as shades of purple in the indigo color of the chakra. The appearance of purple or shades of purple in the region of the chakra indicates extrasensory perception, high spiritual openness, the ability to pick up messages and visions from the universe, a developed imagination, an ability to visualize well, idealism and a meditative and calm way of life.

Both indigo and purple are recommended colors for projecting on the third eye chakra.

The connection between the third eye chakra and the physical body

The third eye chakra is linked to the action of the central nervous system and to all the activities of the brain. It affects the face, the eyes, the ears, and the sinuses.

The eyes are the mirror of the soul. When the chakra is open and balanced, we can use our eyes to observe the person sitting opposite us and receive profound messages about him. The greater the spiritual awareness and openness to receiving non-verbal messages, the deeper the information (or more precisely, the feeling) that is received from looking into the person's eyes. We can see into his mind, and even into his soul.

The eyes represent the way in which we see the world. Our "world-view" (the way we view the world) can be affected by our present life – our childhood, our experiences, by self – and external teaching, by environmental norms, and so on. To the same extent, and often as a result of a direct link, it is also affected by our previous lives, because our soul chose those lives in order to explain previous world-views that were sometimes inhibiting or unresolved.

When spiritual awareness increases and develops, we learn to pay attention to the fact that our world-view, the way in which we choose to see things, is in fact our personal interpretation, seldom objective, and seldom "genuine" from the cosmic point of view. As a result of a subjective view, we attribute to the sights that are revealed to us different interpretations, which sometimes lead to criticism and judgment. We can observe the world benevolently or malevolently. The way we look at it is our internal choice and ultimately reflects the way in which we look at ourselves. Introspection is the foundation of spiritual development and self-awareness. Without introspection, it is not possible to understand the nature of external observation, which characterizes our relationship with others and with life itself.

The reality in which we live is directly influenced by the way we observe things, both external and internal. Since the human tendency is to give meaning to every sight, or seek some kind of explanation for it, we build self-insights. These insights crystallize into patterns. The resulting patterns are projected onto the universe – and whatever we project is realized in our world. For this reason, our world-view is what makes our lives real in this world. In the present, we can create our future by observation and interpretation alone. The more we know how to see things as they are – without the need for personal interpretation in order to "make order out of chaos"; without creating various patterns, some of which are inhibiting (and some supportive); without defining definitions – the more open we will be to accepting the world as it is. Accepting the world as it is immediately leads to accepting ourselves, and creates a situation in which the world accepts us as we are, without so-called external factors (since these factors are the ones that we invite, via our inner beliefs) disturbing the full expression of our personality and soul.

When the person observes the world malevolently, enviously (or is afraid to observe the world), or tends to see it in shades of black, or in black and white only, he may develop visual defects in his physical eyes. By looking into the person's eyes, it is easy to know how he observes the world – critically, fearfully, angrily, or with amazement, love, wonder, and curiosity. The more balanced and open the third eye chakra is (and the same goes for the other chakras), the more balanced and open the way of observing the world will be, thus leading the person to a happy, harmonious, love-filled life. The state of the third eye chakra also affects the ability to see beyond standard vision. It may be expressed in many different things, from seeing details in depth and an ability to observe profoundly via visions and hallucinations (in daydreams, meditation, or dreams), to seeing auras and energy channels, and infinite other aspects of extrasensory observation.

Our ears represent the way in which we listen to the world. When the action of the third eye chakra is involved, it is important to relate to listening not just as listening to sounds that are made or uttered, but rather to the messages that are received from the universe on the one hand, and to the messages that are received from the "I" on the other. Many cases of this hearing being blocked, as a result of all kinds of causes, can be expressed in various levels of hearing defects or various kinds of ear problems – frequently psychosomatic.

Our face is our "visiting card" to the world. When we look at a person's face, we can discover quite a lot about his temperament, because it is revealed on his face: laugh lines in the corners of the eyes, lips that are down-turned from worry or melancholy, a determined eyebrow structure, and so on. The expressions that are acceptable to us, that we tend to use perpetually, are radiated from inside outward to the face, and are imprinted in the memory of the skin cells, and this is how they create a certain kind of "visiting card." Our face signals to people to approach or to go away, it attracts or rejects, it is accepting and open or impenetrable. It can easily express our level of awareness. Since it is our "basket" of expressions, how we accept the world and ourselves is written all over it.

Facial problems can stem from various causes, and the problems themselves are varied, from acne to paralysis of the facial nerve. However, there is often a thread linking the different problems, indicating a need to present something to the world that is not in line with the inner "I," on one level or another. The saying "put on a happy face," actually means "show the world something that is not you at this moment" – in other words, put on a mask. The use of the face to exhibit something that is not the real "me" causes many problems in all layers – physical, mental, and spiritual. One of the first feelings that appears after the third eye chakra has been opened is that there is no danger or disgrace in being myself, and in presenting myself exactly as I am.

The third eye chakra is responsible for the brain and for the central nervous system. Our brain is our personal control room, the switchboard through which all the messages pass. But we are the ones that activate and direct our brain, and not the opposite. All our thought patterns are located in the brain, subject to our authority, whether we are aware of this or not. The brain contains a huge memory bank, a tremendous data bank, and information that can help us in every process. The more open and balanced the third eye chakra is, the more we can utilize the marvelous functions of the brain. We are the activators and programmers of a wonderful super-computer.

As we have written many times already (and repetition is necessary!), we are the ones who create our reality. The thought of today is the reality of tomorrow. At any given moment, we create and shape worlds by the power of thought alone. Recognizing this is a wonderful tool for development in all our layers. One of the things to which the work on opening and balancing the third eye chakra leads is recognizing this power, and understanding its unlimited uses. Because the chakra is the spiritual control center, it parallels the human brain in its function. The enormous potential its development offers are the same tremendous and infinite possibilities that make our brain unique.

When the chakra is not open (and may even be blocked), one of the first noticeable signs is narrow-mindedness. This is an expression of difficulty in accepting truths, experiences, and possibilities that apparently contradict fixed thought patterns that act as barriers against personal ability. The more our mental ability is open, liberated, and prepared to accept the world as it is, without limiting it to the "known" and the "familiar" according to various normative or emotion-dependent thought patterns, the more the ability to accept the best from the world and to be open to the infinite abundance of marvelous experiences increases and is fulfilled in reality.

An imbalance in the third eye chakra is often expressed in headaches, which represent an imbalance in the reception of messages, both internal and external. Sometimes, this expresses a lack of belief in oneself, fear, or self-criticism. When the chakra gets us to understand that we are all souls – clothed in the body and the life of this incarnation – and our lives here are but a dot on the infinite axis of time, self-criticism gradually disappears, and fear gives way to love and confidence in the universe.

Problems of an imbalance in the chakra can sometimes cause nightmares and various nervous problems. Problems in the pituitary gland, the gland that is linked to the third eye chakra, occasionally attest to a feeling of a lack of control of the thoughts, the body, the brain, or life itself. The ideal situation, which symbolizes the openness of the chakra, is the absence of the need for this "control" of life, through understanding that we are the masters of our lives, thoughts, and bodies. There is no need for a desire to control – control does not exist, in the long run – but command and direction do. When we understand that, the need to control disappears, and is replaced by a pleasant going with the flow of life that we create.

The influence of the chakra on hormonal activity

The third eye chakra is linked to the two glands that are located in the brain – the pineal and the pituitary. Very little is known about the pineal gland. It is located at the point of intersection between the (imaginary) horizontal line above the ears and the vertical line that goes up to the crown. It is a small gland, similar in shape to a pinecone. It is not yet known whether or not it is a part of the endocrine system. It releases a hormone-like substance called melatonin, which activates the cycles of the nesting, migratory, and reproductive instincts in animals. In human beings, the pineal gland is in charge of the internal diurnal and nocturnal clock, which affects our hormonal state and our mood. It is also responsible for many other functions. When there is any problem in this cyclicality, feelings of exhaustion, depression, and so on may occur.

The second gland that is linked to the third eye chakra is the pituitary gland. It is located in front of the pineal gland, and serves as a kind of command center that regulates many different functions. The pituitary gland weighs about half a gram, and it is located in a hollow in one of the bones on the floor of the skull. The gland consists of a body and a stem. The stem connects the body of the gland to the hypothalamus. The gland consists of two parts: an anterior part, which contains cells that produce the different hormones; and a posterior part, which serves as a reservoir and a place from where the hormones that are produced in the hypothalamus and transferred to the posterior part of the pituitary are released into the bloodstream. The pituitary is indirectly linked to the limbic system (the emotional center in the brain) through the secretion of hormones that are also linked to behavior and balanced emotions.

The hormones that are secreted by the pituitary gland oversee various activities, as well as the flow of additional hormones. The pituitary secretes two types of hormones:

Tropic hormones – hormones that are secreted from one endocrine gland and activate another endocrine gland.

Somatic hormones – hormones that are secreted from endocrine glands and directly influence the cells of the body.

The pituitary gland can be defined as a "factory" for the production of hormones, both tropic and somatic. Together, the hormones activate the body's endocrine system.

The hormones that are secreted by the pituitary gland involve all layers of physical and emotional existence. The posterior part of the pituitary secretes two hormones that are produced in the hypothalamus into the bloodstream: the first is ADH (antidiuretic hormone), which affects the kidneys and regulates the amount of water that is excreted in the urine. A small quantity of the hormone is secreted after a large amount of water has been drunk, so that the amount of water excreted in the urine increases, and the body gets rid of excess water. A large quantity of the hormone is secreted in states of dehydration, so that the amount of water excreted in the urine decreases in order to prevent the loss of water. It is of cardinal importance in the proper running of the body.

The other hormone is oxytocin, which is secreted in two cases: before and after birth. Before birth, it is secreted in large quantities and causes powerful contractions of the uterine muscles, as well as the opening of the cervix – in other words, labor pains. After birth, it is secreted in order to stimulate milk production during breastfeeding. (The role of the hormone in men is not known.)

The anterior part of the pituitary gland contains cells that produce various hormones. The secretion of all the hormones from this part is regulated by releasing hormones that are secreted from the hypothalamus.

The hormone TSH (thyroid-stimulating hormone) is a tropic hormone that regulates the secretion of the thyroid hormone in the thyroid gland, the importance of which was discussed in the chapter on the throat chakra.

The hormone ACTH (adrenocorticotropic hormone) is a tropic hormone that regulates the secretion of cortisol, a hormone that is secreted from the adrenal gland, which was discussed in detail in the chapter on the solar plexus chakra.

The hormone FSH (follicule-stimulating hormone) is a tropic hormone that is sent to the ovary and regulates egg development, the follicle-producing process, and stimulates secretion of estrogen in women. In men, FSH initiates sperm production in the testes.

The hormone LH (luteinizing hormone) is a tropic hormone whose function is to stimulate the production of the sex hormones in both men and women. In men, it regulates the secretion of the sex hormones from the testicles, and in women, it reaches the ovary and causes it to produce progesterone, to ovulate, and to maintain the pregnancy during the first three weeks.

The growth hormone (GH) is secreted all through life, but its level rises sharply toward the growth spurt (11-17 years), and it is essential for the growth of the bones in children. A lack of this hormone during the growth period causes dwarfism. An excess of the growth hormone, caused by the growth of the pituitary that secretes it during the growth spurt, causes gigantism (a very rare disease that leads to death at a relatively young age because of heart problems). It has been found that the pituitary secretes the hormone mainly at night, during sleep.

As we can see, there is no area of life that is not affected by the pituitary gland – just as there is no area of life that is not affected by the third eye chakra. If it is not open, spiritual life (and, in parallel, physical life which requires the hormonal command of the pituitary gland) will function defectively. To the same extent that the pituitary "commands" all the other hormonal glands, so the third eye chakra has the strongest influence on all the other chakras. When the third eye chakra is open, (even partially, and even if it is not fully balanced), and the rest of the chakras are in a state of imbalance or blockage, there is an overwhelming desire to balance the other chakras. Furthermore, they enable the person to recognize his chakras' state of imbalance, as well as the tools that exist to balance them.

Meditations

The purple ball of light meditation

Perform the meditation in a quiet, calm and well-ventilated place. Use an essential oil burner containing one of the oils that is suitable for stimulating and opening the third eye chakra. Holding an amethyst in your hand can help you enter the meditative state more easily. The meditation should be performed while you are sitting. Take several slow, deep and comfortable breaths, close your eyes and relax your body. Now, see a glowing ball of purple light above your head. While you gaze at the ball of light, concentrate on breathing. Every time you inhale the air, see the purple ball becoming smaller and more concentrated. With each exhalation, pull it into the region of your third eye chakra. When it reaches the size of an eye, approximately, bring it close to the region of your third eye and draw it in with a powerful inhalation. Sit calmly for a few minutes and concentrate on the feeling of the stimulation of the third eye.

Now, evoke a particular event from your memory. It is possible that a certain event will arise naturally at this point. You may not yet have made peace with the event or with the people involved in it; it could be an event that symbolizes something that you yourself have not yet accepted, an insight that is not yet understood, and so on. Bring the event, person or insight into the center of your third eye, which is glowing with shiny purple light. Envelop it in the purple light. If you have any question, ask it now. Continue breathing consciously, and let the insight or the feeling rise up inside you. Enveloping the event in the purple light will enable you to see it in another light – understanding the situation via the third eye, which may expose the true nature of the event.

After practicing this meditation several times, you can apply the projection of the purple light easily to any irksome event, past experience, or confused feeling whose nature you want to understand.

The black dot meditation

This meditation is one of the tools that helps in the process of linking up to the soul and it is useful for balance and support in everyday life. It is a wonderful meditation in states of confusion, bad feelings, anger, depression, fears and phobias or self-doubt. It leads us to an insight and a feeling that there is light in the darkness itself, and we as souls, energetic creatures of light and love, can bring light to any situation that is perceived as dark, by dint of our consciousness. It is possible to perform the meditation seated, standing, or lying down (however you wish, in fact), even when the body is not completely relaxed or when we are not calm. Having said that, if you are not accustomed to entering a meditative state, it is a good idea to relax your body somewhat before beginning the meditation.

Take several deep breaths and close your eyes. Imagine the unpleasant feeling or the distressing situation as a small black dot located at some distance from you. Look at it, concentrate on it. The more you concentrate on the dot, the more its edges turn gray. While this is happening, it slowly increases in size. The gray on the edge of the dot gradually filters into the dot itself, which becomes more and more gray, expanding all the while. As it grows, the gray color, which has meanwhile taken over all the black, fades. The more it grows, the more it fades, and begins to whiten at the edge, which now resembles a circle. Gradually, the circle whitens, expanding, until it blends completely with the white expanse of the background of the dot.

Throughout the process, you must ensure that you are breathing consciously. The feeling after the process is one of relief, of seeing things in proportion, and of confidence in our inner strength to create our reality. On the metaphysical level, you may discover that when you let the black dot become white, the situation or feeling that was bothering you also filled with light, and became lighter and simpler to deal with (and perhaps does not inhibit or disturb you any more).

The seventh chakra

The crown chakra

Sassharta

✸ CHAKRAS ✸

The crown chakra ----------------------

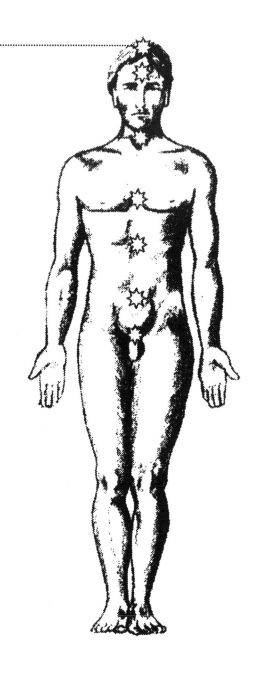

Location of the chakra: The crown of the skull.

Colors: Purple, white, gold, silver.

Symbol: A lotus with 1,000 petals.

Key words: Spirituality, insight.

Basic principles: Pure essence.

Inner aspect: Spirituality, infinity.

Energy: Thought.

Element: None.

Sound: "Om."

Body: The soul, the karmic, causal body.

Body organs linked to the chakra: The cerebrum.

Essential oils: Jasmine, frankincense.

Crystals and stones: Diamond, moldavite, clear quartz, selenite, smithsonite, pyrite.

Stars and astrological signs linked to the chakra: The planets that are associated with the crown chakra are Saturn and Neptune, and the Zodiac signs are Capricorn and Pisces.

Capricorn, which is affected by the force of the planet Saturn, symbolizes introspection, focus on the nature and essence of things, and the transcendence of the material.

Aquarius, which is dominated by the planet Uranus, is linked to the chakra because it symbolizes thinking that is full of inspiration from higher sources, superior knowledge, and developed intuition.

Pisces, which is dominated by the planet Neptune, symbolizes the liberation from limitations, devotion, unity, and recognition of the soul.

The crown chakra is located in the region of the top of the skull, with its petals pointing upward and its stem descending down the central energetic thread. It is also called the peak chakra. The meaning of the chakra's name in Sanskrit, Sassharta, is "the lotus flower with a thousand petals."

The crown chakra is the center of human perfection. It glows in all the colors of the rainbow, but its dominant colors are purple, white, and gold.

It constitutes a limitless bank of knowledge, and the age of its development is infinite. It symbolizes enlightenment and connection to the higher layers of spiritual awareness.

The crown chakra unifies the energies of all the lower energy centers. It links the physical body to the cosmic energetic system and constitutes an electromagnetic center that provides energy to the lower centers. This is the starting point of the expression of all the energies of the rest of the chakras. This chakra is responsible for the link to supreme awareness, for the ability to receive divine and cosmic insights, and for the ability to connect to divine knowledge, to the light, and to universal love. This is the place where we feel "at home." There is no need to "do", no need to "control" reality, no need to think – simply "be" pure essence. This is the place that cries within us, "I am what I am," because of the clear knowledge that this life is just a manifestation of the soul in the body, at a certain time and place. It was chosen by the soul in advance in order to become familiar with reality in a certain way, by recognizing the points of light and "darkness" of existence (which in essence is all light).

Every emotion, every energy, every thought, moves along a vertical line, and the completion of that energy is on that line (that is, the line is an axis whose ends contain complementary "accumulations" of energy). On the same line, fear and love, sadness and joy, anger and self-acceptance, and so on, are located. We can choose to stand on one side of the line, which is fear, or on the other side of the line, which is love. In this way, through awareness only, we can easily turn darkness into light, fear into love, anger into self-acceptance, tension into understanding. From the crown chakra, we begin the journey to that life, which ostensibly constitutes a separation from the divine. From the crown chakra, we experience the unity with the divine that is us. Our personal energy field becomes one of the energies of the universe.

Everything in the universe is energy. For that reason, we can join, affect, and live in every single thing. Every imperfection that appears in front of our eyes is a reflection of the imperfection that we attribute to ourselves. This attributed lack of perfection may be the result of this or other incarnations. From the crown chakra, we learn to accept ourselves in our entirety – as an inseparable energetic part of the universe, as a soul that is experiencing existence in this dimension, as well as in other dimensions of existence.

In this chakra, everything we understand intellectually, cerebrally, and afterwards intuitively, becomes understanding and knowledge. Here, there is no such thing as the "why, what, how, where," but rather knowledge only. The knowledge that comes from the crown chakra far exceeds the knowledge that comes from the third eye chakra, because here we are no longer separated from the object of observation, but rather united with it. We do not see anything in the universe as separate from it. We understand and know that the other is in fact a part of us and a part of the universe, because we are energy that – only apparently – is embodied in a separate body. As a result, devotion, tranquillity, faith, and acceptance are awakened. We are no longer angry, nor do we reject or criticize what we see with the physical eye as being external to us. Rather, we know that that is part of us, that if we feel any objection, it means that we are objecting to what this part expresses inside us, to its reflection in us, as if in a mirror.

When the blockages in the crown chakra are opened and it receives energy fully and perfectly, all the remaining blockages in the other chakras seek to be opened. This is a result of raising our consciousness to a state in which we can, with thought and feeling, bring the nature of the blockage to the surface and liberate it through understanding. All the chakras vibrate at their very high frequencies, and each of the chakras acts as a mirror for the divine nature at its particular level, by expressing its full potential.

When the crown chakra is fully stimulated, we begin to radiate all the cosmic energies that we have absorbed, into the cosmos. From being the ones who are affected, we become the ones who affect the energies, the force in the universe that operates in unison with the universe, "workers" in the service of the divine light, which is us.

The crown center is opened during meditation, even if it is not altogether open on a daily basis. During meditation, the center receives divine knowledge that is later processed and understood via the other centers, and is expressed in thought, speech, and deed.

Harmonious functioning of the crown chakra

There are, in fact, no blockages in the crown chakra. It can be more open or less open, and more developed or less developed. With the opening of the chakra, the person experiences more and more moments in which the difference between external existence and internal existence becomes blurred, and disappears. He experiences many more moments of simply "being," in a state of acceptance – a state that does not involve needs, thoughts, fears, and so on. Consciousness is completely calm, and the person experiences himself as a part of the pure essence that includes everything that exists. The more the crown chakra develops, the more frequent these moments become, until they become a constant feeling of balance and perfect harmony with the self and with the universe alike. The path to enlightenment, which becomes enlightenment itself, is likely to emerge suddenly as a kind of feeling of awakening to reality. The person feels that he is a channel for divine light and is prepared to receive this light at any time and in any form. Personal ego is no longer inhibiting, but rather constitutes a tool for carrying out God's wishes, and is instructed by the soul. There is no more resistance or conflict, but rather acceptance and reconciliation. The person translates the Creator's intention into deed, speech, and thought, and lets it take shape in the physical world. His personal path is the same path that he chose as a soul. The person understands and knows that now every question that arises is not another conflict. All he has to do is ask. He is able to receive the answers from the universe via his soul, which constitutes part of it. He does not feel the need "to do," but rather "is". He does not feel confusion or discomfort; but accepts himself totally, and knows how to see a meaningful sign in everything in the universe. He acknowledges emotions such as fear, anger, criticism, and sadness as additional tools for development and understanding, and knows how to withdraw into himself and examine them in depth in order to become familiar with their source and resolve them. Of course, he does not attribute anything to what is external to him. Statements such as "he annoyed me" or "she hurt me" and so on no longer exist, because the person understands that everything is one and every state of apparent imbalance is a reflection of what needs reconciliation and acceptance inside himself. As a result, he continues developing spiritually. He experiences life as a fascinating game. He understands that everything that happens to him is his own personal choice. It is clear to him that he is the one who chose this life, this body, and these experiences in order to become perfectly familiar with his soul through life in the material world. He understands that matter is just the realization in his awareness of the divine consciousness, and he does not actually exist as matter. When the chakra is open and balanced, the person gains enlightenment and a harmonious, satisfying life.

The characteristics of a crown chakra that is mainly closed

As we said before, there are in fact no blockages in the crown chakra, just states of being more or less open or more or less closed. When the crown chakra is not open satisfactorily, the person feels as if he is a separate, unlinked part of the universe and the essence. As a result, he is not free of fears and conflicts. His energies are not balanced, nor are they in equilibrium with the energies of the universe.

The person may feel that he lacks a vocation, that he is confused, not at one with himself, not fundamentally calm, and full of questions to which he does not know how to get answers. He is constantly bothered by the state of imbalance in the rest of his chakras. He may have a non-supportive perception of his existence, he may feel bored with life, or out of sync with people, situations, animals, and even objects. Fear of death, which stems from a lack of understanding of true existence, is liable to dominate or disrupt his life. He lacks a zest for life, self-confidence, confidence in the universe, and wholeness. He tends to shrug off responsibility for what happens around him, pinning it instead on other forces that he dubs "the others," "the world," and so on, instead of understanding that everything begins and ends with his personal choices. He feels that he has to "do," instead of simply "be" – thus realizing his personal action. He is likely to feel like a plaything in life's hands instead of being someone who has chosen this life. His capacity for spiritual development is small and his true potential is not realized. A very extreme result of a closed crown chakra may be expressed in extreme situations such as coma and death.

The colors of the chakra

The colors of the crown chakra are purple, gold, magenta and white.

Purple is attributed both to the sixth chakra – the third eye chakra, and the seventh chakra – the crown chakra. It is the color with the highest level of frequencies in the color spectrum. It is a color that stimulates inspiration, encourages devotion, opens spiritually, and reinforces meditative abilities. It symbolizes intuition, art, creativity, extrasensory abilities, faith, imagination, and the non-material. It results in the transformation of mind and soul, opens blockages, and leads us to experience the unity of the universe. Purple has good healing abilities, and can be used for the effective treatment of problems in the person's mental body and in cases in which there is a need to stimulate and strengthen the person's spiritual aspect, as well as for stimulating spiritual growth and openness. It also helps treat nervous problems and mental diseases. From the physical point of view, purple assists in weight reduction, stimulation of the spleen, increased production of leukocytes (white blood cells with an essential action in the immune system), halting diarrhea and purification of the blood.

When purple appears in the person's aura and in the region of the chakra in a harmonious and balanced way, it attests to spiritual openness and spiritual abilities, powerful intuition, extrasensory abilities and the ability to pick up spiritual messages and information, as well as to creativity, devotion, idealism, a calm attitude, a meditative and tranquil way of life, and an ability to change and develop. When purple appears in the aura in an unharmonious way, it may attest to religious fanaticism, injustice, obsessive behavior, intolerance toward difference or the "other," use of negative powers and black magic, belief in punishment and retribution, and impotence. When we discern lavender or lilac (light, delicate purple) in a harmonious and balanced way, it can attest to mystical abilities, positive magical powers, and depth of thought. When it appears in the aura in an unharmonious way, it is liable to indicate obsessive behavior, fanatical adherence to ideas, and intolerance of difference.

White is also one of the colors of the crown chakra and of high and pure energy. White light is produced by the combination of all the colors of the spectrum, and white sunlight contains all the colors of the spectrum. In color therapy, healing and meditation, white is sometimes used in order to spark a transformation of awareness and for linking up to the divine energy. White links all the ostensibly different levels of the universe by means of unity, and opens our souls to divine light, to divine knowledge, and to the soul's self-healing ability. This gives rise to a general healing ability, since we ourselves are a part of the entire unity of souls, and every facet of healing that is expressed in us is expressed in the whole universe.

We can often discern the existence of white in the auras of small infants in a harmonious and perfect way, since they are still linked almost completely to the unity of the universe. When we discern white that appears harmoniously in the aura and above the crown chakra, it attests to spirituality, the link to the divine, purity, filling up with light and energy, high and developed intelligence, higher planes of consciousness, elucidation, and the unity of all the colors. When white light appears unbalanced in the aura – that is, in centers in which it is not meant to appear, for example in the center of the lower chakras, or when it looks "dirty" or unharmonious – it is liable to attest to a lack of grounding or to daydreaming, to centers containing too much energy (which can attest to a place that hurts), to a lack of centering, to an unbalanced accumulation of energy, and to receiving energy in an unbalanced and uncontrolled manner.

Gold is one of the colors of the crown chakra. It is the safest cosmic energy for projecting in any situation or case, and is the ultimate healing color. Gold is the color that is suitable for every type of projection, treatment and situation. It is the energy of divine love, and for this reason, it is the safest color for use in color projection. It symbolizes sanctity, purity, and perfect knowledge, as well as spiritual power that is expressed in everything. In color projection, gold reinforces the electromagnetic field and the energies of all the fields, at the same time exerting a beneficial effect on the healing of all the organs of the physical body. It affords a feeling of warmth and comfort, and a feeling of linking up to divine love, and it can be safely projected for treating all physical and mental conditions. When it appears in the aura, it attests to spiritual elucidation and constant openness to receiving the energy of perfect love from the universe. Furthermore, it attests to access to lofty knowledge and sanctification.

Magenta is a color that is the combination of pink and red. It is another color that is linked to the crown chakra, and it can be projected onto the chakra in order to open it. Magenta is considered to be a cosmic color, and when it appears among the colors of the aura, it may attest to a cosmic healing ability. In color therapy, the color is used for treating problems connected to the brain, for instilling joy and vitality in cases of depression, for invigorating, and for treating inflammations and problems in the arteries and kidneys.

The frequencies of the chakra and the energetic bodies

The body that is linked to the crown chakra is the karmic/causal body. This body contains all the information concerning the previous lives of our soul, and its present condition. Linking up to and recognizing the karmic body helps us understand our vocation in this incarnation, the different patterns that stem from the experiences in previous lives, and the feeling of our soul in the present. It constitutes a kind of "forecast" of our soul. By linking up to the karmic body, we can understand what is going on in the present. We can understand why we chose this specific life, and what goal it serves in the perfection of our soul. We can discern if part of our soul is not here at this moment, and call it back and unite with it. Collective memories of humanity, from the past and from the future, also appear in the karmic body. For this reason, it can provide information about the past, present and future of humanity and the universe.

Meditations

Filling up with light

Filling up with light is an extremely powerful energetic tool. Many holistic practitioners, channelers and healers use it prior to and during treatment. However, it is actually a process that is essential for everyone. Filling up with light gives us the central feeling that is expressed by the crown chakra – the feeling of filling up with divine light. We are full of this light all the time, but may not be aware of it. Filling up with light fills us with energy, opens our crown chakra, and, in the second stage of the meditation, strengthens our aura and creates a protective sheath around us.

The meditation should be performed standing up. It does not require much time, and after a few practice runs, can be performed anywhere, any time. It is an excellent technique for intensifying our inner power when we are about to perform tasks that require great effort, before various challenges such as exams and so on, for creating a feeling of power and calmness, after being in energetically, physically and mentally exhausting situations, and in the morning, before beginning the day, in order to be energetic and linked up.

Stand comfortably, back straight, without locking your knees or creating tension in any part of your body. Take care that your muscles are not tense, and if they are, relax them by moving them in loosening movements while breathing consciously.

Close your eyes and take seven deep breaths. On the eighth breath, see golden light descending from above and penetrating your crown chakra. With each inhalation, pull the golden light further inward, so that it envelops every single organ. See it flowing along your spine, in parallel to the organs it envelops in its light. Make the golden light flow forward, to your chest, arms, abdomen, legs, and all the other organs, until you are completely filled with golden light. Once you see yourself full of the golden light, begin to see golden currents coming out of your body and beginning to envelop you in a golden ellipse of light. Spread your arms out sideways, as if stretching the ellipse, increasing the range of its effect and its protection. The golden light is above you, at your sides, behind you and beneath you. The golden ellipse looks as if it is slightly flexible. Now tell yourself that anything that does not support you on the outside cannot penetrate the protective ellipse. See anything that does not support you on the inside as being "sprayed" out through the ellipse, dissolving, and returning to the source where its energies will be converted into supportive and loving energies. Sketch the outline of the ellipse around you with your hands. When you pass your hands over the surface of the ellipse, you can feel a warm or prickling energetic sensation in your palms.

At this point, you can complete the meditation with an expression of thanks to the source, to the divine power that provides you with support and protection. You can also go on to the third stage of the meditation: In your mind's eye, evoke the people you love, or any person to whom you wish to send golden light, love, support and protection. You can also visualize the planet Earth itself in your mind's eye, in order to transmit love to it and to Mother Earth. See the tremendous light that is enveloping you going on to filter into the picture of the person you evoked in your imagination. You can see him in your head or standing beside you, wrapped in golden light that is becoming his own golden, supportive and protective ellipse. Conclude the meditation by expression your thanks to the universe.

The "face" chakra

✿ CHAKRAS ✿

The *"face"* chakra ———————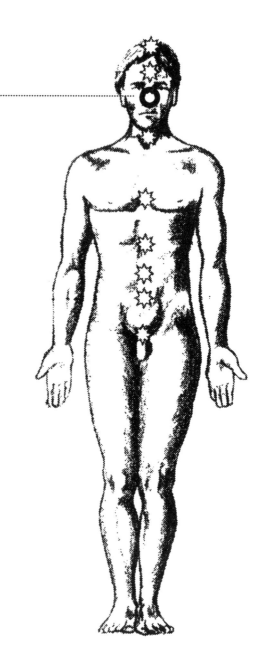

Location of the chakra: The posterior region of the head, parallel to the height of the nose.

Colors: Brown, ocher, olive green.

Key words: Resonance, duality, healing, instinct.

Element: Damp earth.

Sense: Smell.

Body: The causal (lower instinctive) body.

The connection between the chakra and the physical body: The chakra provides general protection by picking up messages and signals. Furthermore, it is linked to the right hemisphere of the brain and to posture, the skeleton, and the spine, as well as to the general balance of the body and the self-healing and regenerative capacity.

Glands: Adrenal glands.

Essential oils: Cedarwood, rose, geranium.

Crystals: Snowflake obsidian, fossils, peacock rock, dendritic agate.

The "face" chakra (whose name varies according to the source) is a chakra about whose existence there is general consensus, although opinions differ as to its function. It is one of the two "additional" chakras that we felt we had to mention, because of their great importance.

The petals of the "face" chakra are located in the region of the nose. Positive energy concentrates in the stem, which is located in the area of the lower curve of the head, by reacting to the "ancient brain" (which existed before the brain divided into two hemispheres). It is responsible for the person's feeling of harmony with his surroundings and with nature by strengthening the link between him and nature – the mineral, plant, and animal kingdoms, as well as the landscape around him. This chakra links us to the instinctual system that has existed in man since the days of the ancient brain, a system that protects him from danger and enables him to assess events through eyes that are in perfect harmony with nature.

As a result of the action of the "face" chakra, we can identify the messages of the ancient instinctual system that operates in us. The instinctual ability – the same ability that enables animals to sense an earthquake several hours or even days before it happens, or sense the approach of a storm, and so on – also exists in human beings. However, because of a lack of awareness of this system, its signals are ignored, so much so that the ability to use the chakra is lost. Today, when people react to this ability and undergo experiences in which they are saved from danger, they tend to attribute their deliverance to "luck." This is not the case, however. Every event is a creation that transmits the signals of its existence even before the event itself occurs. In the same way as a little child refuses to do something that he senses is dangerous, because of a primordial fear, we too can pick up the signals of the emergence of a life-threatening danger before it happens – if our instinctual system is developed.

Another action that is attributed to the "face" chakra is communication with our collective subconscious. This is similar to the "The hundredth monkey" theory, a scientific theory that concerns human beings as well as animals. According to this theory, when a monkey on a certain island initiates some action – for example, washing a potato in the stream before eating it – this action will be learned by another monkey, and thus the rest of the monkeys on the island will learn it from one another. According to the theory, when one hundred monkeys on the island learn this action (one hundred represents the optimal percentage), all monkeys everywhere will recognize and perform this particular action.

Through the energetic communication system, which connects us to one another, we actually know all the human actions that are performed. Our collective subconscious stores the sum total of human actions from the very inception of humanity until now. We can see how the theory works nowadays. Many people choose to develop the awareness of what has happened beyond recent centuries of human existence. More and more people pick up these messages and also begin to feel the need and desire to develop their spiritual awareness. More and more people understand that the way the world and reality are perceived today is an illusion, and this number is gradually increasing.

The "face" chakra is also responsible for our link with nature, with our natural cycle, the seasons, animals, elements, minerals, and plants. In the past, people were closely connected to the natural cycles. They would eat seasonal foods (without extending the natural growth period of the plants) – so that they ate the plants that were most supportive for them in the particular seasons. Similarly, they did not interfere in the growth cycles of the animals they raised, which permitted them to make the most of those cycles in a natural way. Today, things are different. Fruit and vegetables are grown in hothouses and undergo various processes and methods that ensure their availability year-round, and animals are raised on breeding farms, in pens and chicken-runs, without taking into account their cycles of growth, birth, and death. This lack of consideration for the cycles of nature is likely to be to the detriment of the human race.

Many people do not perceive the members of the natural kingdom – the minerals, plants, animals, earth, and sea – as a part of us, so that a kind of covert "racism" is forming. This racism stems from the perception of the natural kingdom as different from us, and therefore it can be enslaved and abused. Many people find it difficult to understand that people and nature are one. Because of this distorted and dangerous perception, humanity is now trying to invent things that will prevent the destruction of the earth as a result of human deeds, and these inventions sometimes continue to distort the ways of nature. This dangerous cycle deprives us of the natural freedom to be part of nature if we do not utilize our behavior, deeds, and awareness to prevent the ongoing destruction. Of course, ignoring the natural cycle of the universe affects our health, both individually and collectively.

The "face" chakra also activates our natural powers of healing. Through a connection to nature, certain people, whose chakra is developed and balanced, can sense the various healing powers that exist in the universe. They can therefore heal by using these powers in the different layers: healing through medicinal herbs, minerals and crystals, spending time in places that have beneficial energetic powers, and so on. In addition, each one of us has a natural healing ability. The ability to influence the autonomic nervous system, which is crucial for our health, is a function of our awareness, as is the ability to develop a good sense of the condition we are in and soothe it or stimulate it as necessary.

The "face" chakra is principally linked to the right side of the brain, which has a substantial influence on our self-healing ability, and on our ability to bring our body back into balance and to stimulate the properties of renewal and recovery in our organs. This ability is, of course, connected to our ability to connect to nature and balance ourselves through direct contact with it.

The "face" chakra, unlike the seven other principal chakras, is not linked to a particular sound or Sanskrit sign. Its frequencies are not directly linked to its location, but rather occur between those of the base and sexual chakras. Its element is linked to the elements of those two chakras. The sense that is attributed to it is the same as the one that is linked to the base chakra, and the glands are the same ones as those of the solar plexus chakra.

Harmonious functioning of the "face" chakra

The balanced and open state of the "face" chakra is expressed as a good connection and link with the world of nature. It affords the person a high awareness of the animal and plant worlds, and the ability to experience nature in all its forms through peace and connectedness. When the chakra is open and balanced, the person has healthy and good instincts that tend to be relatively higher than the ones that are seen normally. Sometimes, the person can feel instinctively when a certain place is unsuitable for him, or contains some kind of threat. The person knows himself and his natural rhythms. His state of health is good – he does not succumb to disease easily. If he does get ill, his body tends to recover quickly, sometimes even without medical intervention, because he is aware of his condition and can take care of himself by resting and by fulfilling the needs of his physical and emotional health.

Unharmonious functioning of the "face" chakra

When the "face" chakra is unbalanced, the person tends to detach himself from nature and to be unaware of the cycles of nature, their influence on his life, and his own natural rhythm. He is liable to wear himself out with work, to be insensitive to his body, to get into unnatural and dangerous situations needlessly and through imperception, and may even succumb to stress-related diseases such as hypertension. Moreover, in the case of disease, the healing abilities of the body, as well as the awareness of the activities that support the health and renewal of the body, are minimal, and the diseases tend to be more prolonged. The person has difficulty being aware of things that are beyond regular, basic existence – home, work, money, errands, and so on. His sensitivity is lower, and he is not sensitive to his surroundings. Sometimes this is expressed in a negligent and disparaging attitude toward nature. In extreme cases, when the other chakras are not balanced either, the ego is unbalanced, and the third eye and crown chakras are practically not open, the person is liable to behave destructively toward the environment. He is likely to perceive the human race as superior to nature and as having the right to abuse and crush nature, thus constantly harming the universe.

The link between the "face" chakra and the physical body

The "face" chakra is linked to the general health of the body, to the awareness of the body's state of health, and to physical balance, mainly in its manifestation in posture and the condition of the skeleton. It activates the ability to listen to the body and to discern which actions support it and which actions inhibit it, as well as which foods and lifestyle suit the person. Finding the personal rhythm of action that is unique to the person enables him to divide his energy correctly and usefully. He knows when he is most alert during the day, when he is physically and mentally active, or when he needs rest in order to restore his strength. He knows what his inner rhythm is, and can adjust his way of life accordingly, so that he feels energetic and full of vitality the whole day through. Because the "face" chakra raises our consciousness about our body, it also activates the ability to feel the approach of a disease, and to act accordingly in order to support our body wisely.

Our body perpetually renews itself, and undergoes processes of renewal and wear and tear. "Old" cells die, and young cells replace them. The more open and balanced the "face" chakra is, the greater the body's ability to renew itself. This ability is important mainly in situations of recovery from wounds or surgery.

The hara chakra

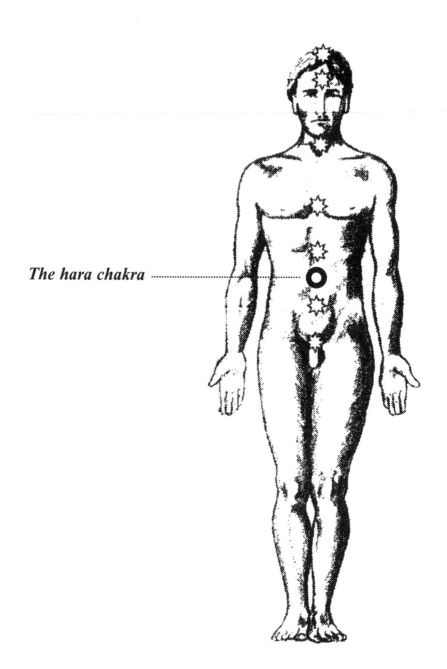

The hara chakra

Location of the chakra: Between the sexual chakra and the solar plexus chakra.

Colors: Peach, silver.

Element: Granite.

Key words: Power, vitality, healing, balance, regeneration.

The connection between the chakra and the physical body: The chakra elevates the body's power and energy and increases its resistance and its capacity to adapt. Its state of openness affects physical balance.

Essential oils: Frankincense, apricot, peach.

Crystals and stones: Sunstone, stephanite, vulpinite.

The hara chakra is a chakra about whose existence and functions there is general consensus. It is the second of the "additional" chakras that we felt we had to describe because of their great importance.

The hara chakra is not located "inside" the physical body, but rather in the body's aura. It is linked to the other chakras – the main ones and the secondary ones – by energy lines. It is located in the place where Chinese tradition places the source of chi, the person's life energy. In certain people, this chakra is alert and active, while in others it is dormant or almost completely closed.

The hara chakra is the source of powerful energy. In order to stimulate it and reinforce its activity so that it is felt most significantly, it is extremely important to balance and stimulate the solar plexus and sexual chakras so that they can bolster its action. When these chakras are balanced, open, and supportive, the hara chakra can open up and let its energy flow into the body and aura. The energy of the hara chakra affords us much more power, a higher energetic level, excellent resistance and adaptive abilities – all of which enable us to feel harmonious and natural in every situation because we can match the energetic condition to ourselves.

The opening of the hara chakra affords us vitality – the ability to accept every moment as it comes, as a result of perfect harmony; to live life moment by moment – in the present. Many people tend to live in the future: "What I have to do in order to achieve…," "If I do X, I will get Y…," "If I had…," and so on. Similarly, many people tend to live in the past: "If I had done this and that…," "If I had gone to X and told him Y…," and so on. As a result, they do not make the most of the present; it is not felt; it is lost. The energetic movement vacillates continuously between wishes for the future and regrets about the past. The marvelous feeling of accepting things as they are, the experience of each moment as it comes – the perfect realization of the reflection of our thoughts, desires, imaginings, and wishes in the present – is lost. Vitality means living each moment to the full, being totally immersed in the here and now. It is not over-activity – an unnatural condition that depletes our energy banks – nor is it watching from the sidelines without getting involved.

Harmony and balance are two of the hara chakra's additional functions. When the chakra is active and balanced, it helps us feel balanced physically, emotionally, and spiritually. The balancing action of the hara chakra is also significantly expressed in the balancing of our posture. For this reason, it is important to focus on it when treating postural defects. On the other hand, ensuring correct posture through awareness of the energetic condition that is caused by correct posture helps open and balance the hara chakra. The hara chakra helps us recognize our strength. Strength means the ability to move things, to activate, to do – physically, mentally, and spiritually. The condition of the hara chakra affects the way in which we perceive and accept our strength. The more we believe in the strength within us, the more perfectly and powerfully it can be implemented.

The hara chakra's power is important and very helpful in the treatment process as well. In various Eastern techniques, such as Shiatsu, a great deal of emphasis is placed on work from "within" the hara center. When the work is done from within this center, the physical energies are balanced and flow harmoniously, so that the therapist can administer lengthy treatments without feeling exhausted, lacking in energy, or pain. Furthermore, the work from within the powerful hara center helps us avoid drawing the recipient's symptoms and pains into ourselves. However, the hara chakra does not only have an important role in healing others (although healing "others" is actually an incorrect concept. With every person we treat, we are actually treating ourselves, so that every healing procedure is ultimately self-healing), but is of great significance in self-healing as well. Developing the hara chakra and connecting to it during the course of self-healing and guided imagery substantially increases our self-healing energies. In addition, the hara chakra causes the flow of regenerative and renewing energies that help us not only cure diseases and problems, but also bring about physical, emotional, and spiritual renewal of organs and conditions.

The hara chakra is also responsible to a great extent for our equilibrium – physical and symbolic – which is expressed in all areas of life. This is the equilibrium that exists between us and our world, in harmonious giving and receiving.

Harmonious functioning of the hara chakra

When the hara chakra is open and balanced, the person feels strong and healthy. He is aware of his personal power, sure of himself and his strength, and can consequently easily accomplish every task along his personal path. The belief in his inner power is a tremendously powerful tool that enables him to invite the perfect experiences he wants to have into his life – experiences that support him along his path. He is not afraid of not realizing his dreams (a fear that would cause him to experience a reality in which his dreams are not fully realized) – but rather lives, creates, and acts out of his unique path. He notices that the universe reacts to and realizes his perceptions, imaginings, thoughts, and so on, perfectly. When the hara chakra is open and balanced, self-awareness rises substantially. The person also feels physically strong. He does not attract diseases energetically. If he falls ill, he recovers quickly. Often, because of the good regenerative capacity of his body, soul, and spirit, no traces or "traumas" of the disease remain in his system.

The balanced and open state of the hara chakra engenders a feeling of general equilibrium. This is expressed physically, by maintaining a strong and healthy spine (from the emotional and the "environmental" point of view, too). Everything is in a state of balance. Giving and receiving, which occur in all the layers of life and the universe, flow harmoniously, and no lack or excess are created (threatening to lead to non-positive feelings). The person has a good level of self-awareness, and can thus give himself the time and care he needs for healing – from every point of view. He can give himself what he needs physically, mentally, and spiritually, and is aware that he deserves it. His vitality is high, he enjoys every moment, and the people around him are positively affected by his presence.

Unharmonious functioning of the hara chakra

Unharmonious functioning of the hara chakra, or blockages in it, is frequently expressed in a low level of vitality, or in a state of believing that the vitality level is low – that is, the person does not acknowledge his physical, mental, or spiritual strength. As a result, he avoids performing various actions, or feels that he requires the help of others to perform them. The unbalanced action of the chakra can cause an incorrect distribution of energy. This could be expressed in a large expenditure of energy on marginal issues, or performing actions that waste a tremendous amount of energy, leading to a feeling of weakness and a lack of energy.